1898:

The SPANISH-AMERICAN WAR

Told with Pictures
by IRVING WERSTEIN

Cooper Square Publishers, Inc.
New York   1966

This Book is for
Dr. Cyril Solomon
and Ann Simon

973.8
W
Ln

First Edition

Copyright © 1966 by Irving Werstein
Published by Cooper Square Publishers, Inc.,
59 Fourth Avenue, New York, N. Y. 10003

Book designed by S. Sigaloff
Library of Congress Catalog Card Number: 65-21406

Printed in the United States of America

HAVANA INTERLUDE
February 15, 1898

The USS Maine, under full steam, heads towards Havana, in February, 1898.

Captain Charles Sigsbee, U.S. Navy captain of the 6,682-ton second class battleship, U.S.S. *Maine*, stood on the bridge, enjoying a late evening cigar.

The *Maine* bobbed gently at her anchorage in the harbor of Havana, Cuba, where she had been moored for almost three weeks. That night, Tuesday, February 15, 1898, Sigsbee had no hint anything out of the ordinary would soon happen.

As he had done every night since the *Maine's* arrival at Havana, the skipper made a thorough inspection tour of his ship; all guard posts had been checked, officers of the watch queried, gun crews posted. Despite the tranquil, starry Cuban night, the U.S.S. *Maine* maintained full alert; Captain Sigsbee, well aware of the reasons that had brought his ship to Cuba, was leaving nothing to chance.

Leaning on the bridge rail, he glanced across the water towards the city of Havana; from the ship, he could see twinkling lights and buildings outlined against the skyline. It was hard to believe that Havana only recently had been torn by riots and that the island of Cuba—"Pearl of the Antilles"—writhed in the agonies of revolution and bloody oppression. Deep in the jungles and the passes of the Sierra Maestre mountains, rebel bands carried on savage guerilla war against their Spanish rulers. (Cuba had belonged to Spain for more than three centuries.) Over the years there had been many insurrections and uprisings as Cuban patriots strove to free their island from Spanish domination. Each revolt had been crushed with great cruelty and ruthlessness.

In the United States, most people were sympathetic to the rebels, who were called *insurrectos*. By 1898 American public opinion was strongly against Spain.

The rending explosion that shattered the USS Maine on the night of February 15, 1898, is graphically captured in this vivid painting of the eventful moment.

Now, with civil war again raging across Cuba; with *insurrecto* bands burning sugar mills and plantations; with rioting and fighting in and around Havana, the American consul Fitzhugh Lee, had appealed to Washington for help. On January 12, 1898, he cabled the State Department that "American lives and property were endangered by the disorders in the city . . ."

The U.S. government responded quickly, sending to Havana the U.S.S. *Maine* and the light cruiser U.S.S. *Montgomery* on an officially labelled "goodwill visit." By January 25, the two American war ships were moored in Havana harbor. The pretext of "goodwill" was maintained; Spanish officials held a reception for the ships' officers and enlisted men. Sailors off the *Maine* and the *Montgomery* went ashore on liberty to crowd waterfront bars, restaurants and shops.

Outwardly everyone seemed friendly and cordial under the surface smoldered Spanish resentment at the presence of the *Yanqui* warships. However, for three weeks, nothing unpleasant occurred. There were neither riots nor plantation burnings; revolutionary

(Upper right) Crew of the Spanish cruiser, Alfonso XII, lower boats to rescue survivors of the stricken Maine. Note U.S. battleship burning in background as tugs and harbor craft race to the scene.

Captain Charles Sigsbee,
skipper of the USS Maine.

activity had simmered down and that balmy February night, it was so quiet that Captain Sigsbee, at his place on the *Maine's* bridge, could hear the distant strains of music drifting across the harbor from waterfront cafes about a mile away.

Sigsbee glanced about in the moonlight. He saw, some 300 yards to port, the shadowy bulk of the Spanish cruiser, *Alfonso XII*, riding easily at anchor. Farther out sat an American freighter, the *City of Washington*. Moored about 100 yards to starboard was the *Maine's* escort, the U.S.S. *Montgomery;* at various other moorings were the ships of other nations: here a British merchantman, there a Dutch steamer, a Belgian cargo vessel or a German passenger packet.

Sigsbee lingered a bit longer; despite the lull in violence ashore, conditions might change at any moment. He puffed on the cigar and sighed. The world was certainly in a mess, all the killings and suffering in Cuba; the threats and rumbles of war: a Spanish warning to the U.S. to keep out of Cuba; arguments between Great Britain and Germany; France and Italy in a headlong arms race and actual warfare in the Balkans.

Fitzhugh Lee, U.S. Consul at Havana.

"Abandon ship!" he ordered.

A bugler sounded the call and surviving crewmen leaped overboard. All forward lifeboats had been splintered by the explosion and only three at the stern were in usable condition. Ships anchored nearby were showered with flaming debris from the *Maine* but they quickly lowered rescue boats to pick up the men floundering in the water.

Sigsbee was rescued by a launch from the *Alfonso XII* which carried him to shore as the *Maine* went down. She sank in five minutes, settling in thirty feet of water with only her superstructure poking above the surface. The ship burned more than four hours wracked by internal explosions as flames reached her ammunition lockers.

The fo'c'sle, where the ship's crew was quartered, had taken the brunt of the initial blast; as a result, casualties were high. Many men had been killed instantly, others drowned when the ship sank. Of the *Maine's* 350-man complement, 260 enlisted personnel and three officers were lost. Up to that point, it was the worst disaster in U.S. naval history.

When Sigsbee reached shore, he hurried to Consul Lee and after a hasty consultation with him cabled a report to Secretary of the Navy John D. Long. Aware that the tragedy might have serious consequences, Sigsbee cautioned: "Public opinion should be suspended until further proof of the disaster's causes . . ."

On the deck below, a sailor trod a sentry post, the moonlight glinting off his bayonet. Sigsbee glanced at his watch. It was 9:30 P.M.

After a last lingering pull on the cigar, he flipped the butt overside, watching its fiery arch into the water. The captain left the bridge, clambered down the iron stairs that led to his quarters on the foredeck and entered the cabin. Removing his spotless, starched white uniform blouse, Sigsbee sat down at his desk and started a letter to his wife.

The stillness of the room was broken only by the tread of a sentinel, the humming of the ship's dynamos and the pen scratching on the paper. He had scrawled only a few lines when suddenly, without warning, a great blast rocked the ship. The lights blinked out. A second explosion shook the *Maine*.

Acrid smoke billowed from the ship's depths. Sigsbee staggered half-stunned from his cabin, choking in the thickening fumes. Men stumbled by carrying fire axes and hose; flames leaped from every part of the stricken *Maine*.

Dragging himself up on deck, Sigsbee finally reached the bridge. One glance at the seething flames which engulfed the stricken vessel from stem to stern convinced him she was doomed.

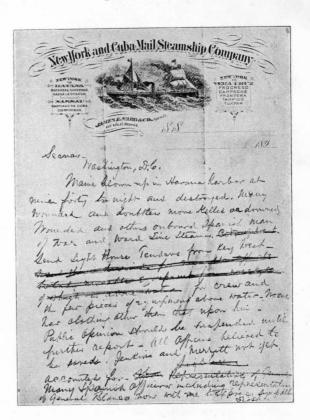

Original message cabled to Secretary of the Navy John D. Long by Captain Sigsbee.

However, William Randolph Hearst's *New York Journal* and Joseph C. Pulitzer's *New York World* observed no such restraint. *"Remember The Maine! We Demand Vengeance!"* thundered the *Journal* while *The World* bellowed: *"War Now! Avenge The Maine!"*

The "Yellow Press" claimed to have "inside" information that proved the *Maine* had been blown up by "Spanish" agents. Sensational, but unfounded, charges blamed Spain for the catastrophe.

These stories were eagerly swallowed by an avid public and the clamor for war against Spain rose on every side, although cooler heads pointed out that the explosion might have been the result of gas seeping from the *Maine's* bunkers. This was a common cause of explosions on ships at that time.

But the voices of reason were drowned by the raucous cries of warmongers and jingoes. Even before any certainty that Spain was guilty, the U.S. took the road to war with that nation . . . .

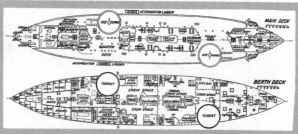

Cross sectional drawing of Maine shows crew's quarters where casualties were greatest when underwater device such as mine shown exploded. Headline in New York Journal **whips up war spirit as mast of sunken Maine juts out of water in Havana harbor.**

BACKGROUND OF CONFLICT
1823-1898

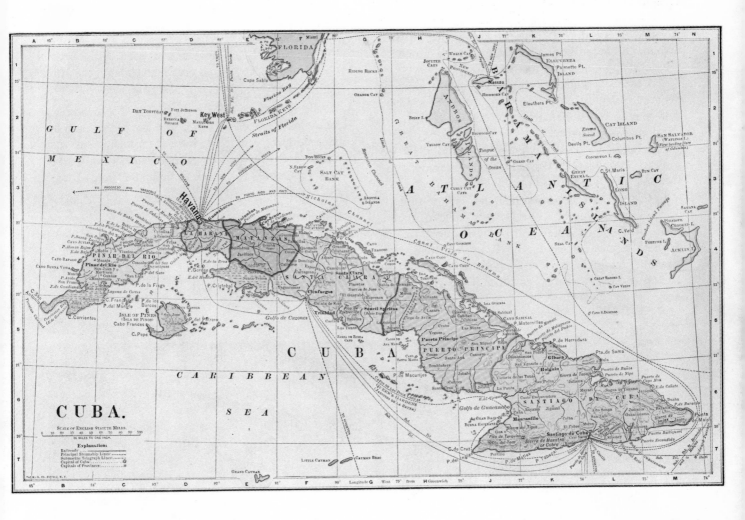

In 1898 the average U.S. citizen had long accepted the idea that a war with Spain was inevitable. For years newspapers such as the *New York Journal* and the *New York World* whipped up mass sympathy for the Cuban rebels. These dailies and others around the country ran lurid "eyewitness" accounts of Spanish atrocities in Cuba.

Murders, kidnappings and assassinations were vividly described by "on-the-spot" reporters whose stories bore Havana datelines although the authors seldom came any closer to that city than Tampa, Florida.

A favorite subject of Hearst's and Pulitzer's imaginative reporters was the mistreatment of "beauteous Cuban Señoritas" by cruel Spaniards. A purple yarn, written with all stops pulled out, dealing with the fate of a "helpless maiden" not only stirred the wrath of

American readers, but also raised the paper's circulation.

These stories, whether outright fabrications or based on half-truths, inflamed the American public against Spain. Enrique Dupuy de Lôme, the Spanish Minister to the United States, vigorously protested about an especially grisly tale from Cuba which disclosed the massacre of some *insurrectos* by Spanish troops. The victims, according to the *Journal* were ". . . youths in their adolescent years . . . Their number included several girls, whose raven tresses were matted with blood . . ."

According to the reporter, ". . . my eyes blurred with tears of rage . . . at the sight . . ." His readers reacted in the same manner as did the Spanish Minister who met a *Journal* editor at a social function.

"What are you trying to do?" demanded de Lôme. "You know that story is an outright lie. Do you mean to start a war?"

"No, Mr. Ambassador. We're just trying to round up a few more readers," the editor grinned.

The same newspaper involved de Lôme in an ugly scandal by printing a letter the Ambassador had written a friend in which the diplomat undiplomatically called U.S. President William McKinley: ". . . a weak man and a bidder for the admiration of the crowd . . . besides being a common politician . . ."

U.S. public indignation seethed. Mass meetings condemned Spain for "insulting our beloved president" and many voices clamored for action against "the slanderous Spaniards . . ."

The de Lôme letter, although unflattering to McKinley, certainly reflected only the ambassador's private thoughts and had nothing to do with Spain.

In the midst of the storm the letter had aroused, the fair-minded editor of a rival paper created another furor by asking: "Where and by what means did the *Journal* acquire access to the Spanish Ambassador's personal mail? Were illegal methods used by Mr. Hearst and his character assassins? If so, what are the authorities going to do about it? Senor de Lôme, after all, enjoys diplomatic immunity. . . His rights should be protected . . ."

The *Journal's* defense was to become offensive. A front page editorial blasted the opposition editor as a "traitor" for "impugning the integrity of this great American newspaper . . ." Senor de Lôme tendered his resignation at once and the entire affair probably would have been forgotten except for its unfortunate timing; the de Lôme letter was exposed by the *Journal* on February 8, 1898—and only a week later, the *Maine* was blown up.

It did not take much for the Yellow Press to hint a connection between de Lôme and the *Maine* tragedy. But Americans as a whole needed no incitement; they already hated Spain. The calamity in Havana harbor merely provided the spark to light the "fires of war."

Cuba had been on the American mind since the United States became a nation. One of the Founding Fathers, Thomas Jefferson, wrote: "Cuba's addition to our confederacy is exactly what is wanted to round out our power as a nation to the point of its utmost interests. . ."

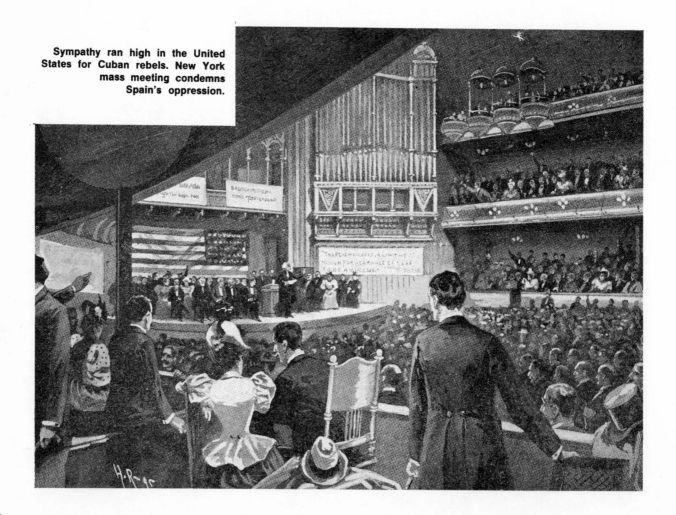

Sympathy ran high in the United States for Cuban rebels. New York mass meeting condemns Spain's oppression.

John Quincy Adams, had stated, in 1823, while serving as Secretary of State under President James Monroe:

"It is scarcely possible to resist the conviction that the annexation of Cuba to our Federal Republic will be indispensible to the continuance and integrity of the Union itself . . ."

This statement was made at a time when Spain's South American and Caribbean colonies were in revolt. It was feared by President Monroe that Great Britain might take advantage of the Spanish predicament to seize that country's most important Caribbean possessions—Cuba and Puerto Rico. To forestall this, he issued the Monroe Doctrine which pledged the United States against such changes in the Western Hemisphere.

Although Great Britain had shown no intentions of taking over any Spanish holdings in the Carribbean, Americans generally mistrusted the British. "If anyone does any land-grabbing down there (the Caribbean) it's going to be Uncle Sam," a New York Congressman said bluntly.

In the decades that followed, many crises developed over Cuba. While Great Britain made no move to take over the "Pearl of the Antilles", Cubans rose in one bloodily suppressed insurrection after another.

On several occassions revolutionaries attempted forays to Cuba from Key West or Tampa. The first time, Nacisco Lopez, a Venezuelan filibuster or soldier of fortune, gathered some 600 men at Key West and was stopped from invading Cuba only by the intervention of American authorities.

Three years later, Lopez tried again. He sailed from Key West and on August 11, 1851, landed at isolated Bahia Hondo with a mixed force which included Hungarian republicans, German socialists, Cuban rebels and American adventurers. Lopez had promised his men that, once ashore, they would be supported by massive uprisings throughout the island.

However, this support did not materialize and the invaders were either slain in battle or captured and executed.

Warfare without quarter raged in Cuba. Rebels (left) fire on Spanish troops from tree-top ambush.

Corpses of executed insurrectos lie in row as warning to Spain's enemies.

Bahia Hondo where Narciso Lopez and his followers were killed or captured in bungled invasion of Cuba on August 11, 1851.

(By a quirk of history, the 1961 Bay of Pigs affair ended in an almost similar manner a century later.)

The fate of the Lopez expedition did not stop the filibusters nor dampen the ardor of Cuban revolutionaries and their American sympathizers.

More filibuster groups formed on American soil, causing grave tension between Madrid and Washington. To retaliate for U.S. toleration of Cuban revolutionary activity within its boundaries, Spain began seizing American shipping in waters off Cuba.

This created a serious emergency on February 28, 1854, when Spanish police in Havana boarded the American merchantman *Black Warrior* and imprisoned her crew on a charge of "violating customs regulations."

Never had Spain and the U.S. been so close to war. The menacing situation inspired three American diplomats, Pierre Soulé, James Mason and James Buchanan —the U.S. ambassadors to France, Spain and Great Britain—to meet in Ostend, Belgium, where they drew up a manifesto which stated in part:

"... Our past history forbids that we should acquire the island of Cuba without the consent of Spain unless justified by the great law of self-preservation ... After we shall have offered Spain a price for Cuba, far beyond its present value, it will then be time to consider the question: 'Does Cuba in the possession of Spain seriously endanger peace and our cherished Union?' Should this question be answered in the affirmative, then by every law, human and divine, we shall be justified in wresting it from Spain. . ."

The so-called Ostend Manifesto was both hailed and damned in the U.S. Southern cotton growers strongly favored it, for they saw a chance to extend slavery and their holdings if Cuba were made an American possession.

Sugar planters also favored the Manifesto. Conversely, abolitionists and the majority of Northerners condemned the plan although everyone agreed that something should be done about Cuba.

In the raging argument over the controversial Manifesto the Cuban people were overlooked. Nobody asked whether they wanted the U.S. to rule the island. Apparently the Cubans did not relish changing one master for another. *"Cuba Libre!"*—"Free Cuba!"— remained the battle cry of the revolutionaries and that meant freedom from both Spain and the U.S.

The Ostend Manifesto was soon lost in the growing antagonism between the North and the South. Although when Buchanan became president in 1856 he several times mildly suggested that Congress ought to consider offering a price for the troubled island, the outbreak of the American Civil War made Americans forget Cuba's problems; there was turmoil enough at home . . .

Drawing (left) shows rebels pledging loyalty to the revolution as color guard holds Cuban flag.

Insurrectos **raiders**
put sugar plantation
to the torch.

Oddly, during the four years 1861-65 when the U.S. was rocked by its civil war, Cuba enjoyed a brief period of peace. For several years, a liberal government ruled in Spain and it seemed that great reforms would be granted to Cubans. But political upheavals unseated the Madrid liberals before any changes could be made; unrest simmered and men whispered darkly of impending revolution in Cuba. However, by 1868, another shift in government brought joy to the islanders; Spain was governed under a new constitution. This enlightened document gave freedom of speech, universal suffrage and other privileges to the Spanish people and at the same time decreed that Cuba, Puerto Rico and Spain's large Pacific colony, the Philippines, should have complete equality with the mother country.

Unhappily, these rights were never implemented. The men who ruled the colonies—the *peninsulares*—simply ignored the progressive points of the constitution. In Manila and Havana all remained as it had been.

The results of such highhandedness were predictable. A social volcano erupted; once again Cuba burst into revolutionary flames. On October 10, 1868, an *in surrecto* named Carlos Céspedes raised the flag of revolt. Blood once more stained Cuban soil. This uprising against Spain was destined to last ten years; it all but devastated the verdant island.

The Ten Years' War was marked by ghastly atrocities on both sides. From the beginning, the Spanish controlled the coastal regions, the towns, highways and populated centers, while the *insurrectos* ruled in jungle and mountain. Sugar plantations were laid waste; thousands died of bullets or disease; Cuba's economy was almost ruined. Had Spain been able to send 40,000 or 50,000 troops, the *insurrectos* could have been crushed, but the homeland was torn by a civil war between two royalist factions and there were no soldiers to spare.

To make up for the lack of troops, the *peninsulares* resorted to ruthless force. Men, women and children were shot down without mercy; entire villages were

Mounted partisans rally in rugged Sierra Maestre mountain stronghold after returning from foray.

put to the torch for sheltering rebels; time after time homes were raided without reason and the residents executed on the merest suspicion. All this was done on the orders of a Spanish general, Juan Balmaceda, who had been given the mission of crushing the rebellion.

Spain's brutal tactics evoked widespread sympathy for the *insurrectos* in the U.S. Mass meetings were held in large cities; money for food, medical stores and arms were collected. Dozens of Americans sneaked into Cuba and fought with the rebels.

Once again Madrid retaliated by ordering the seizure of merchant ships flying the Stars and Stripes. American seamen were arrested, beaten, tortured and imprisoned. A public clamor rose for American action against Spain; the wrathful American people demanded an end to the illegal capture of U.S. shipping.

Congressmen and Senators made warlike speeches.

"Have we grown so weak, so craven, that we stand meekly by while the black hearted tyrants who rule Cuba spit upon our flag, throw our citizens into prison and seize our ships? Have we forgotten how to defend Old Glory?" cried a Michigan senator.

"No! No!" roared his colleagues.

From various sections of the floor and the galley came blood-curdling rebel yells. The old antagonisms between Northerners and Southerners were forgotten; men who had worn the Blue and the Gray only four years earlier, now rose as one to protest Spanish outrages against Americans.

Madrid, still hamstrung by domestic troubles, wisely sought to mollify the angry Americans. The Spanish government apologized, released prisoners and ships, and, on several occasions, paid indemnities. Gradually, tempers cooled off in the U.S. but the clouds of war were never fully dispelled.

Gun runners smuggle weapons and ammunition ashore for insurrectos **at isolated cove somewhere on Cuban coastline.**

The Virginius Incident -
October 1873

The side-wheeler Virginius **sailing off Cuba.**

Four years later, a dangerous incident almost ended the uneasy peace. On October 31, 1873, the American sidewheel steamer, *Virginius,* was pursued and captured off Cuba by a Spanish gunboat, *Tornado.* The *Virginius* jettisoned the cargo of arms and supplies she was hauling for the *insurrectos.* Also aboard were more than 100 Cuba-bound filibusters coming to join the insurgents.

The *Virginius* and her passengers were brought ashore at Santiago, where the *commandante,* General Juan Burriel, summarily labelled all on the American vessel "enemies of the state" and sentenced them to death.

On November 4, Burriel ordered three Cubans and one American from the *Virginius* to be executed. Three days later 37 prisoners, including the ship's skipper faced firing squads. A number of American citizens and British subjects were in that luckless group. The U.S. and British consuls at Havana protested bitterly but met with official indifference. The following day, November 8, a dozen captives, among them three Americans, went to their doom at Burriel's command.

News of the executions set off angry demonstrations in the U.S. The New York Journal set the pace with a headline that shrieked *"We Demand An Eye For An Eye!"* In Washington, a mob formed outside the Spanish Embassy and was dispersed at bayonet point by a detachment of marines.

President Ulysses S. Grant called an emergency meeting of his cabinet; lights burned late in the White House as the Chief Executive and his advisors discussed what steps to take. As their leaders convened, the public, most of the press, clergymen of all faiths and prominent individuals demanded stern counter measures.

What Americans did not seem to realize was the miserable state of the U.S. armed forces. The Army numbered barely 20,000 officers and men scattered at posts across the land. In 1873, the Army's main function was to police the frontier, chase renegade Indians and guard key points. It was poorly armed, undermanned and hopelessly inadequate.

The Navy was in no better shape; Civil War ships lay rotting and rusting at anchor in undefended harbors. If ever a nation was unready for war, the United States filled the bill.

Unprepared or not, the *Virginius* incident called for action. President Grant ordered Secretary of Navy George M. Robeson to mobilize a flotilla of warships at Key West ". . . for possible punitive action . . ."

Robeson did his best, but the ships he collected were described by a journalist as "floating scrap heaps." The U.S. armada was comprised of rust streaked iron clads and creaking frigates that had not weighed anchor since 1865.

While the Yellow Press screamed, *"We'll Make Spain Rue The Day!",* more responsible newsmen

of-war, *Niobe,* was despatched from Jamaica to Santiago. With loaded guns, she raced into the harbor; her captain, Sir Lambton Loraine, warned that he would open fire if further executions took place.

Awed by Great Britain's seapower, the Spanish immediately released all British subjects among the survivors. Americans, however, remained in captivity. At last, after several weeks of correspondence between Madrid and Washington, the Americans were set free. Secretary of State Hamilton Fish demanded a large indemnity, a 21-gun salute to the American flag and the return of the *Virginius.* He also asked that General Burriel be punished. Madrid complied with every point but the last. Instead of punishment, the officer was given a decoration and a promotion. The Spanish were well aware that the U.S. could do nothing without a navy; the Madrid press openly sneered at America and Spain had a free hand in Cuba.

A strong movement got underway in the U.S. to rebuild the Navy. But it was to take ten years before anything was done. In 1883, prodded by Secretary of the Navy, William C. Whitney, Congress appropriated funds to modernize the Navy. Under Whitney, overage ships were scrapped and replaced by fast, heavily armed, steel-plated cruisers and battleships. The naval building program brought the U.S. from twelfth place to third position in maritime strength by the end of the 19th century ...

wondered what Robeson's makeshift fleet could do against first-rate Spanish gunboats based at Havana and Santiago. "No reasonable person can expect our venerable vessels to stand up in battle," said the *St. Louis Post Despatch.*

Fortunately, there was no need for the decrepit American naval squadron to set sail. The British sloop-

Crew members of the Virginius **face firing squad in Santiago, Cuba, as townspeople look on. Executions were carried out on orders of General Juan Burriel (above)** commandante **of Spanish troops at Santiago.**

REVOLT IN CUBA 1895

Cuban patriot Maximo Gomez led 1895 revolt against Spain in Mantanzas region.

Handsome Antonio Maceo was one of the young insurrectos who rose against Spanish tyranny in Manzanillo province during the 1895 revolt.

In 1878, a moderate Spanish general, Martinez Campos, finally negotiated a fair settlement of the Ten Years' War. He met with Vincente Garcia, who then led the *insurrectos* and, at Zanjon, Cuba, on February 10, 1878, signed a treaty which guaranteed all Cubans freedom of speech, press, assemblage, public education and many other reforms.

For seventeen years, Cuba enjoyed an era of peace during which the island's economy flourished and the ravages of the long war gradually disappeared. However, the time of well-being soon ended; Spanish benevolence rubbed thin. Under Don Emilio Calleja, the Spanish Captain-General of Cuba, the old, oppressive ways were restored.

Corrupt officials pocketed funds earmarked for schools, hospitals and roads. Graft was rampant. Crooked authorities mistreated Cubans. Anyone who protested too strongly was arrested, beaten, tortured or murdered. Conditions grew so intolerable that the people began striking back; policemen and soldiers were assassinated; night raiders put sugar plantations to the torch and once again rose the battle cry: *"Cuba Libre!"*

On February 24, 1895, the banner of revolution was unfurled. Everywhere in Cuba fiery patriots rallied around ardent young leaders. In Manzanillo Province, Antonio Maceo led a band of bold *insurrectos;* near Mantanzas, Juan Gomez and several hundred followers took the field against Spanish tyranny.

Soon the smoke from burning *haciendas* and sugar can fields billowed upwards to blacken the sky. The *insurrectos* set clever ambushes and harrassed the Spaniards with torch, bullet and *machete*.

Madrid recalled Calleja and sent General Martinez Campos, the Peacemaker of Zanjon, in his stead. But the man who had ended the Ten Years' War could

Hit-and-run rebel marauders attack Spanish owned sugar plantation on outskirts of Havana. Note raider shot from saddle by defensive fire.

Not all Cubans joined insurrectos. Here, a Spanish officer (mounted) drills recruits for special anti-insurgent battalion. Unit is made up of Cubans.

not stop this latest rebellion. Gomez and Maceo launched attacks from every side, driving Campos's troops back to Havana, where the bedeviled general begged Madrid for more soldiers. The capital itself was no sanctuary from *insurrecto* forays. Often, for days at a time, rebel raiders isolated Havana by cutting telegraph lines, blowing up railroad bridges and setting numerous fires in the city's suburbs.

After a few months, Campos could take no more and resigned saying: "I have failed . . . but no force can crush this rebellion . . . There is a spirit at work here which defies the bayonet . . . I predict that soon this island will be lost to us forever . . ."

The Madrid authorities branded Campos "a weakling, fool and coward . . ." Queen Regent Isabella replaced him with General Valeriano Weyler, whose vicious deeds against the *insurrectos* during the Ten Years' War had earned for him the nickname *El Carnicero*—The Butcher.

He soon lived up to his reputation. A week after arriving at Havana, Weyler issued stringent decrees to control the populace. Violation of The Butcher's ordinances brought an immediate death sentence; his murder squads carried out their orders with fanatical fervor.

General Valeriano Weyler, the Governor of Cuba, was appropriately nicknamed "El Carnicero"—The Butcher—for vicious methods he used to suppress rebellion.

Weyler's predecessor, General Martinez Campos, had helped end a ten-year-long Cuban rebellion in 1878. But the Insurrection of 1895 raged on despite every effort at mediation by Campos.

Queen Regent Isabella of Spain poses with her young son, King Alfonso XIII. It was at Isabella's orders that Weyler went to Cuba and tried to drown the rebellion in blood.

It soon became a common sight to see dead *insurrectos* lying by the roadside or bodies dangling from trees. Weyler's men executed, without compunction, young boys and girls merely suspected of aiding the rebellion. A British reporter saw three high school girls callously shot down in the heart of Havana.

But even Weyler's terror could not break the rebellion. As Campos had said, there was a spirit at work which defied the bayonet. The *insurrectos* responded vigorously to The Butcher's brutality. Fighting flared throughout Cuba during 1897. The rebels attacked at dozens of points, never losing heart, even though Antonio Maceo was killed.

As the *insurrectos* were battling Weyler to a standstill, The Butcher earned for himself many thousands of enemies in the U.S. He was labelled by a newspaper as "the man most Americans despise."

One incident especially enflamed Americans. Weyler had resumed the practice of stopping American ships in the vicinity of Cuba to search them for arms, filibusters or *insurrectos*. The steamer *Olivette*, flying the American flag, was boarded outside Havana. A pretty Cuban girl, Evangelina Cisneros, accused of acting as a rebel courier was taken into custody.

The *New York Journal's* man in Havana, Richard Harding Davis, filed a routine story about the occurrence. His dispatch contained nothing sensational, but publisher William Randolph Hearst seized upon the tale and embellished it.

19

When Davis's report appeared in the *Journal* on February 12, it was enhanced by a large engraving showing a frightened girl cowering unclad before three lecherously leering Spanish officers. The drawing was the work of Frederic Remington, who would one day become one of America's outstanding artists, just as Richard Harding Davis later won fame as a war correspondent.

The effect of the picture and the vividly written story was electric. Clergymen denounced "bestial Spanish defilers of womanhood." A Southern reader of the paper proposed that a group of "chivalrous gentlemen should journey to Cuba for the purpose of lynching Weyler . . ." In New York, toughs stoned the Spanish consulate. Effigies of The Butcher dangled from lamp posts.

Even after Remington admitted the drawing had not been made "On The Scene" as captioned, but in the newspaper's office, anti-Spanish ferment raged unabated. Davis protested that his story had been rewritten in the home office. (Actually, Señorita Cisneros had been searched by a female inspector in privacy and then released.)

This made no difference to the *New York Journal*. The paper neither printed a retraction nor tendered an apology. "After all," declared a Hearst spokesman, "it would be difficult to exaggerate conditions in Cuba. We merely took a little dramatic license. Our editors were only serving the interests of the public. Americans hate Spain, so we gave them something to stew about."

Star journalist, war correspondent and author Richard Harding Davis posed for this sketch by his wife, Cecil Clark Davis.

Frederic Remington's controversial sketch of an incident aboard a steamer in Cuba aroused American anger. Even Remington's admission that the scene was fictional did not silence anti-Spanish clamor. The drawing appeared in Hearst's New York *Journal*.

Cartoonist lampoons William Randolph Hearst, publisher of the **New York** Journal and the San Francisco Examiner. **Hearst's papers led campaign for war on Spain.**

New York Public Library Picture Collection

SPANIARDS SEARCH WOMEN ON AMERICAN STEAMERS

As the Cuban struggle went on, scores of adventurers, trained in the U.S., landed on Cuban shores to join the *insurrectos*. Shiploads of guns, paid for by Americans, reached the insurgents. Officially, Washington took a dim view of these goings on.

During the closing days of his administration, President Grover Cleveland sternly admonished: "This government views with disfavor . . . all such illegal attempts by its nationals to interfere with the affairs of a friendly foreign power . . ." However, in referring to the stoppage of American vessels by the Spaniards, he warned. "The United States is not a nation to which peace is a necessity . . ."

On March 4, 1897, William McKinley succeeded Cleveland in the White House. He announced that his administration frowned upon American citizens helping the insurgents.

Instead of abating, the flow of men and arms to Cuba increased daily and a Spanish official there cynically stated, "Every time the *insurrectos* raise their flag, the band plays 'The Star-Spangled Banner' . . ."

All at once the situation in Cuba unexpectedly turned better. Spain's reactionary Prime Minister, Canovas Castillo, was assassinated in Madrid. His successor, Praxedes Mateo Sagasta, head of the Liberal Party, took steps at once to end the Cuban revolt.

He offered the *insurrectos* broad concessions, demonstrating his good faith by removing Weyler and putting a Liberal, General Ramon Blanco, in The Butcher's place. Sagasta also announced a new constitution for Cuba, one granting the islanders a good deal of self-government. Weyler's repressive decrees were rescinded when Blanco arrived in Havana. He ordered a general amnesty, unconditionally freeing all political prisoners. Spain's new stance should have brought peace but the day of enlightenment had arrived too late. The *insurrectos* no longer wanted crumbs from Spain.

"We demand *independencia*—independence—and will settle for nothing less," a rebel leader declared. "Our war cry was, is and always shall be *Cuba Libre!*"

Thus, though Blanco held out the olive branch, there was no peace. *Insurrectos* still stalked the hills and came raiding from jungle hideouts; flames crackled in the night; men died and blood stained the verdant foliage.

This was war to the death.

General Blanco's liberal régime faced a threat even more menacing than that from the insurgents. The *peninsulares* resented bitterly the reforms he had instituted. They sabotaged him in every way and plotted to overthrow his administration by force.

Matters came to a head on January 12, 1898, when several thousand *peninsulares,* led by army officers,

William Mc Kinley, 25th President of the United States, hoped to settle the Cuban crisis by peaceful means, but the destruction of the USS Maine ended all chance of averting war with Spain.

Prime Minister Praxedes Mateo Sagasta, head of the Spanish government, was a liberal and progressive leader. He vainly sought a peaceable solution to his country's friction with the United States. But Sagasta could not prevent the Spanish-American War.

gathered in a noisy demonstration outside Blanco's official residence.

The huge throng soon turned into an ugly mob and a riot broke out. Wild crowds raced through the streets, looting, burning and beating passersby. Several Americans were mauled and American-owned property suffered damage.

At this point, Consul Fitzhugh Lee sent out his call for help:

> "Uncertainty exists whether Blanco can maintain order . . . Americans and their interests are endangered . . . Ships must be sent . . ."

It was in response to this plea that the *Maine* and the *Montgomery* sped from Key West to riot-torn Havana. When the battleship's anchor splashed in the waters of the harbor, the *New York Journal* ran a banner headline: *"Our Flag Is In Havana At Last!"*

Publisher Hearst personally penned the leading editorial that day. He wrote: ". . . everything is now in readiness for the final act of the drawn-out ordeal of Cuba . . . It is hoped that the climax may not be long delayed . . ."

Hearst rushed his ace artist, Frederic Remington to Havana to "draw pictures of the fighting and the action . . ." After a week or so, Remington cabled his employer: "Everything is quiet. There is no trouble here. No war . . ."

Hearst purportedly replied:
"You furnish the pictures. I'll furnish the war . . ."

Meanwhile, completely unnoticed in the excitement over Cuba, the U.S. Navy was on the move in an area far from home shores. Across the Pacific, in the Philippine Islands, a revolution against Spain's iron rule had been raging for months. This struggle was almost completely disregarded in U.S. political, military and naval circles; while the average American probably never had heard of the Philippine Islands.

However, the attention of at least one influential man was drawn to those distant, war-ravaged islands.

A platoon of Spanish soldiers pose for a snapshot in the field during a seek-and-destroy operation against rebel units hiding in the mountains.

In fierce action the insurrectos overwhelm a Spanish field artillery battery southwest of Havana as American and Spanish diplomats argued the question of peace or war between those two countries.

22

On January 3, 1898, Commodore George Dewey— a crusty, 60-year-old sea dog, with a fine Civil War combat record—had assumed command of the Asiatic Squadron. Dewey and Roosevelt were friends; in fact, the Commodore owed his latest assignment to the young Under Secretary. Because Roosevelt knew he could count on Dewey's co-operation and tact, the future President jeopardized his own political future. Acting without permission from Secretary of the Navy Long, Roosevelt cabled Dewey to move his ships from Nagasaki to Hong Kong and there prepare them for "any exigency."

If Dewey had hesitated or questioned Roosevelt's unusual orders, Teddy's public career might well have ended abruptly; Secretary Long was furious upon learning what his subordinate had done, but, since Dewey had acted promptly, he was already at sea, beyond recall.

He was Theodore ("Teddy") Roosevelt, the dynamic Under Secretary of the Navy. The brash Roosevelt, bristling with energy and vigor, was convinced that war between Spain and the U.S. might be postponed but not avoided.

Spurred on by this convictions, "Teddy" pored over his maps to find the potential enemy's weakest spot. This he believed to be the Spanish Navy's Asiatic Squadron, comprised of obsolete, rusting warships based at Manila Bay.

The U.S. also had an Asiatic Squadron—four firstrate cruisers and several gunboats berthed at the port of Nagasaki, Japan. The American flagship, the six-year-old 5,000 ton *Olympia*, was considered by experts to be one of the world's finest fighting ships.

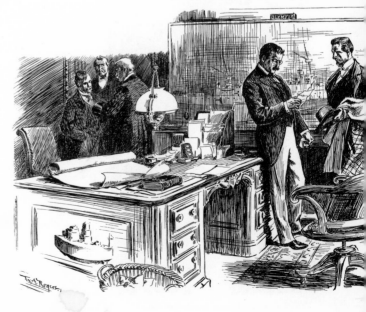

George Dewey, 60-year-old commander of the
U.S. Asiatic Squadron was a tough, hard-hitting
sailor, who rose from rank of Commodore
to Admiral after winning victory over
Spanish fleet at Manila.

John D. Long, the U.S. Secretary of the Navy.

The commodore shrewdly surmised that should there be war with Spain, his just combat mission would be to attack Spanish ships at Manila. Upon his arrival at Hong Kong, he began preparing for this assignment, by putting his squadron in shipshape condition, ready for action at a moment's notice.

Senator Henry Cabot Lodge, distinguished Massachusetts solon was leading spokesman for administration in Spanish crisis.

By coincidence, Dewey reached Hong Kong on January 25, the same date the *Maine* anchored off Havana. The prospect of war loomed large. As propaganda drums beat more strongly, tension became almost unbearable. Daily, the yellow press described Cuba's plight in stories of famine, misery and death.

"*There's Blood On Our Doorstep!*" the *Journal* shrieked.

In less flamboyant style, Senator Henry Cabot Lodge of Massachusetts wrote a friend in London: "We now have a battleship in the harbor of Havana . . . There may be an explosion any day in Cuba which would settle a great many things . . ."

At the time, Senator Lodge did not realize how prophetic were his words . . .

24

THE CLOUDS GATHER
February-April 1898

The gleaming white 5,000 ton cruiser Olympia served as Dewey's flagship in the U.S. Asiatic Squadron. The Olympia was considered one of world's finest fighting ships.

President William McKinley acted with restraint in the hectic days after the sinking of the *Maine*. Instead of heeding the ranting press, the war talk and the over-zealous patriots, who were demanding satisfaction from Spain, the President appointed a commission, headed by Captain William T. Sampson, to investigate the causes of the disaster.

McKinley flatly stated, "I shall take no position until the full report of the commission is in my hands."

The President, walking a tightrope between the peace faction and the so-called "War Hawks," urged the people, "to remain calm and to withhold any judgement . . . until all the evidence is in . . . Ameri-

cans traditionally believe a man innocent until proven guilty . . . Let us do the same for Spain . . . However, should it be shown that the Spaniards did commit this foul deed . . . those responsible for spilling American blood shall feel our righteous wrath . . ."

The harried President still hoped to avert war by diplomatic means such as cessation of the Cuban revolt. He ordered the U.S. Minister at Madrid, Stewart Woodford, to help negotiate a cease fire between the Cuban *insurrectos* and Spain. McKinley believed that a satisfactory settlement of the revolt would stifle American clamor for war.

The Spanish Squadron of the Philippines contained obsolete vessels such as shown here: (from l. to r.) Don Antonio de Ulloa, Velasco, Isla de Cuba, Castilla, Don Juan de Austria **and the** Isla de Luzen.

The U.S. Asiatic Squadron had modern, sleek ships including the cruisers: Boston, Baltimore, Olympia and Raleigh (l. to r.) plus the destroyer Petrel and Concord (background) and the picket boat Mc Culloch (background).

As the war clouds gathered, President McKinley held frequent meetings with his cabinet (above). Four distinguished officers, Captain Chadwick, Captain Sampson, Lieutenant Commander Maria and Lieutenant-Commander Potter (below, left) formed a committee to investigate the Maine disaster. Portrait (right) is Admiral Alfred Mahan, author of book Influence of Sea Power, which strongly influenced American expansionist sentiment.

Although conservative men such as Senator Mark Hanna (below, right) counselled against waging war on Spain, inflamatory cartoons (above) in the daily press kept the war fever at high pitch in the United States.

The Spanish government was willing to give up the struggle in Cuba on almost any terms short of independence, but the *insurrectos* would not even consider an armistice.

"Why should we quit fighting now?" an insurgent leader asked. "Soon the *Americanos* will be on our side and with them behind us, we'll get everything we want including *Cuba Libre!*"

The President met much opposition in his "peace" crusade. His most outspoken critic was Teddy Roosevelt. The belligerent Under Secretary of the Navy openly sneered, "McKinley has the backbone of a chocolate éclair!"

At a formal state dinner, Roosevelt shook his fist under the nose of Ohio's Senator Mark Hanna, the President's chief advisor, and roared, "Damn you! We'll have war for the freedom of Cuba in spite of you and your gutless bunch!"

Roosevelt's attitude was indicative of the country's spirit. War fever mounted daily. According to one commentator, "We're itching for a scrap with anyone . . . and Spain will do fine!"

This bellicose American attitude was a symptom of the deep-seated changes that had taken place in the U.S. since the close of the Civil War. Until 1865, Americans generally had been content within their own borders; protected from the outside world by two wide oceans, the U.S. had flourished behind its isolationist barrier. With the exception of the Mexican War (1846-48) the nation seldom had undertaken any international adventures.

Few Americans gave serious thought to annexing land outside continental U.S. However, by the closing decade of the 19th Century, the country became obsessed by a desire to obtain "real estate" and "plant the flag" in other parts of the world. Until then, the idea of the Stars and Stripes flying over some Pacific island, in Africa or Asia, had seemed ridiculous.

Admiral Pascual Cervera y Topete (right) commanded
the Spanish Atlantic Fleet with its ancient battleship
Pelayo (above), speedy torpedo boat destroyers (left,
center) and the fairly new cruiser, Infanta Maria Teresa.

28

The powerful U.S. Navy had many modern warships. Among
the best were: the cruiser Marblehead (3); the battleship
Massachusetts (13); and the cruiser Cincinnati (18).

The truth was that Americans were beginning to grow restless behind their own boundaries; the frontier was gone and business needed new markets. In 1876, the U.S. enjoyed a fairly brisk export trade; but within 20 years, it rose to $200,000,000 annually and was a mainstay of the national economy.

It became obvious to statesmen, politicians, industrialists and commercial interests that one key to American economic growth was the extension of foreign markets. During this same period Great Britain, France, Germany and Italy staged a neck-and-neck race to take colonies; they carved up Africa, hacked out spheres of influence in China and gobbled up loose islands in the Pacific Ocean. The U.S. was far behind in this contest for empire.

Imperialist-minded Americans did not like being left in the lurch. In 1890, Captain Alfred Mahan wrote a book entitled *The Influence of Sea Power* and at the same time advocated a strong U.S. merchant marine, and a powerful two ocean navy with bases all around the world. Mahan also wanted American colonies to provide markets and raw material.

This concept pleased most Americans. They supported the vision of U.S. merchantmen laden with American-made goods covering the world's trade routes; and they enjoyed the idea of two mighty U.S. navies guarding not only home shores, but also the outposts of an American empire.

For the first time in the country's history, people turned their gaze outward. By the '90's, Americans discovered with a shock that those natural bounties they had so long taken for granted were being curtailed; thick forests were denuded of trees, grasslands and pasture lands had been prodigally wasted.

Mushrooming factories were spilling out of the cities and onto farming land. Only a few years earlier, a man merely packed his belongings and headed west if he wanted elbow room; but that freedom no longer was available. The American continent had been conquered and now the conquerors had to find fresh worlds.

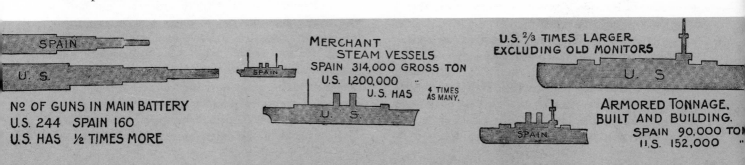

SPAIN

U.S.

Nº OF GUNS IN MAIN BATTERY
U.S. 244   SPAIN 160
U.S. HAS ½ TIMES MORE

MERCHANT
STEAM VESSELS
SPAIN 314,000 GROSS TON
U.S. 1,200,000 "
U.S. HAS   4 TIMES
AS MANY.
SPAIN
U.S.

U.S. ⅔ TIMES LARGER
EXCLUDING OLD MONITORS
U.S.

ARMORED TONNAGE,
BUILT AND BUILDING.
SPAIN 90,000 TON
U.S. 152,000 "
SPAIN

Aware that expansion would bring the U.S. onto a collision course with other nations seeking to widen *their* horizons, American imperialists still launched a fervent campaign. This was a time of superpatriotism, jingoism and nationalism. The flag was displayed on every pretext. Every school child had to recite a pledge of allegiance before class each morning.

As this overly stressed patriotism rose to mass frenzy, Senator Shelby M. Cullom of Illinois bluntly stated: "America wake up! It's time we grabbed some colonies of our own . . . We *must* get hold of additional property even if we have to start a war for it!"

The first strides along the road to empire taken by the U.S. came only seven years after the Civil War. The native chief of the Samoan Islands gave permission for the U.S. to build a naval base at Pago Pago on Tutuila Island.

Great Britain and Germany also cast an eye on the Samoans. A naval war, with the U.S. on one side and Great Britain and Germany on the other seemed imminent; the three nations mobilized warships off Samoa and, without doubt, an engagement would have taken place except for a sudden hurricane which wrecked all the vessels.

The intervention of nature allowed an interval for discussion and the three countries settled their differences amicably. For a time, the Samoan Islands were jointly owned by the U.S., Great Britain and Germany; in 1899, the British pulled out, after dividing up their holdings between the other powers. Germany lost her Samoan possessions in World War I and the U.S. remained master of the pleasant islands.

Another major move for imperial power came when the U.S. was granted the right to establish a fortified naval base at Pearl Harbor near Honolulu, Hawaii. A U.S. inspired revolt overthrew the Hawaiian Queen Liliuokalani in 1893. On July 4, 1894, Hawaii was proclaimed a republic and four years later, July 7, 1898, became a territory of the U.S.

Samoa and Hawaii only whetted expansionist appetites; business men complained that while Great Britain, Germany, France and Russia were actively securing good places for themselves in China, American commercial interests had been left out in the cold.

A leading industrialist declared: "We demand justice and fair play! American business has as much right in China as that of any nation. Let's go in and get a slice of the pie. We're paying taxes to maintain a big navy. Well, let's use it!"

Senator Albert J. Beveridge of Indiana, an expansionist spokesman, stated in a Senate speech:

". . . We are a conquering race . . . we must obey our blood and occupy new markets, and, if necessary, new lands. American factories are making more than the American people can use. American soil is producing more than they can consume. Fate has written

Senator Albert J. Beveridge of Indiana, a brilliant, handsome young orator, was the outstanding spokesman for U.S. imperialists and an exponent of colonialism. He urged a war of conquest and land-grabbing at a time when colonialism was on the rise among the great world powers such as England, France and Germany.

our policy for us . . . The trade of the world must and shall be ours . . ."

McKinley, who had been elected with the enthusiastic support of Big Business, delivered an inaugural address on March 4, 1897, which upset his backers. They believed the President was an ardent expansionist who would fight to gain new territory. On that March morning, McKinley disillusioned followers: "We want no wars of conquest; we must avoid the temptation of territorial aggression . . .", said the incoming President.

Despite the tone of the inaugural address expansionists, led by Senator Henry Cabot Lodge of Massachusetts and firebrand Teddy Roosevelt, doubled and redoubled their demands for a "bigger, richer, stronger America . . ."

Shortly after McKinley had been sworn in, a group of Republican Congressmen visited the President to suggest that the U.S. Navy occupy several groups of islands in the South Pacific.

They specifically mentioned the Carolines, the Marianas (then called the Ladrones) and the Marshalls. In response McKinley snapped: "I will not put up with this jingoistic nonsense! Nor will I lead this nation into war to gain some remote, disease-ridden tropical islands . . ."

The President wanted amity and peace but he was out of step with the people. Some Americans, notably the famous humorist, Mark Twain, took an anti-war stand. Twain wrote: "The American people have grown "war happy". For no sane reason, war suddenly seems romantic, glamorous and glorious to them. They think war is bands, parades, glittering uniforms and cheers. Bosh! War is sheer unmitigated horror! War is Hell, as General Sherman once said and there are

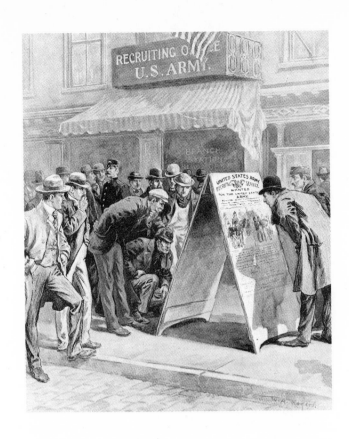

plenty of men around who can testify to that . . ."

Americans did not choose to remember that war was Hell. The national temper was such that a western Congressman, writing home after the *Maine* disaster, could say: "I tell you this means war with the Spaniards . . . even if the Commission clears them of all blame, it will make no difference . . . The people are bound to have a war and that business in Havana Harbor is excuse enough to start one . . ."

Civilians (upper left) study U.S. Army recruiting poster in New York City at outbreak of war. Volunteers are given a check-up by army doctors at a reception center (upper right). The war spirit flamed high and even old Civil War veterans tried to join the colors (lower left). Train carries recruits to camp as friends and relatives give them a hearty send-off (lower right). It was an oft repeated scene in the U.S.A.

On March 28, 1898, the report of President Mc-Kinley's *Maine* Commission of Inquiry, was made public. After an investigation lasting 23 days, Captain William T. Sampson, the Commission chairman, released the results of that body's intensive work. The report concluded:

"In our opinion . . . the Maine was destroyed by a submarine mine which caused the partial explosion of two or more of her forward magazines . . . The Court has been unable to obtain evidence fixing the responsibility for the destruction of the *Maine* upon any person or persons . . ."

The Commission, despite its earnest labors, solved nothing and muddied an already confused situation. After the reports were given out, controversy about the *Maine* flared afresh. Some naval experts believed a mine, torn loose from the floating minefield which formed Havana's coastal defense, had drifted against the ship.

Many maritime designers and naval consultants rejected the mine theory and insisted that coal gas seepage had caused the initial explosion. (This hypothesis received support in 1912 when the *Maine* was raised from the harbor mud. An examination of the rusting hulk showed the battleship's bow plates were buckled outwards indicating the first blast had taken place internally.)

In the emotion-charged atmosphere of 1898 Americans abandoned logic and fact. A climate of prejudice and bigotry was at large in the land. To narrow-minded Americans every Spaniard was a "dago"—a derogatory name for all Latins except Mexican—who were called "greasers". Native-born Americans, prejudiced against foreigners, treated them with scorn and contempt.

During the '90's the U.S. experienced great waves of immigration from southern and eastern Europe plus swarms of penniless Irish. Hungarians, Italians and Jews, who came out of Polish and Russian ghettoes, tramped off steamers by the thousands. They crowded into big city slum tenements; some drifted to other parts of the country, but wherever they went, the newcomers met intolerance and unfriendliness.

Americans, born of forbears who had come from Europe only a few generations before, spurned the "greenhorns"—a slang term for immigrants. Anglo-Saxon Protestants hated Catholics, both Christian sects detested Jews and most whites despised Negroes.

It was a paradox that a nation riddled with so many cross currents of bias should be willing to fight for the sake of Spanish-speaking, dark-skinned Catholic Cubans. This contradiction was discussed at the time by a writer:

"We Americans are a contrary bunch . . . We don't like foreigners but invite them here. We treat them bad at first . . . but after a while don't give a hoot where a man came from . . . just so long as he pulls his own weight. . . Our main trouble is that we grew too fast . . . and we're still learning that democracy means everybody, no matter what his name, origin, religion or color . . ."

The drive for war picked up speed, although Mc-Kinley and a few men around still tried to apply the brakes. In Madrid, Ambassador Woodford met daily with Premier Sagasta.

The Spanish Prime Minister sought desperately to avert a conflict. Spain's strength and wealth had been drained by the long-drawn insurrections in Cuba and the Philippines. The once mighty Spanish Navy was obsolete and dilapidated; the morale and efficiency of the 24,727 officers and sailors who manned the fleet had corroded along with the ships.

On the other hand, the U.S. Navy was at its peak, thanks to Secretary Whitney back in 1883. Among the Navy's 86 fighting ships were the world's newest and best equipped craft.

Five more big battleships were nearing completion at the Philadelphia navy yards and would soon be

William Jennings Bryan, the "Boy Orator", the "Great Commoner", who had run for president on the Democratic ticket in 1896, cast aside his pacifist views and joined a Nebraska regiment.

ready to join a fleet with a personnel of 15,425 officers and men including 2,000 Marines.

Undoubtedly, Premier Sagasta's peaceful attitudes stemmed from the sad shape of Spanish naval power. He was also aware of his army's deplorable state. Having a potential 183,000 man strength in wartime, the Spanish Army lacked discipline, training and leadership. Armed with a German-made Mauser rifle, an excellent weapon, the average Spanish soldier had never been trained to use or care for it properly.

Despite its inadequacies, the Spanish Army greatly outnumbered the U.S. Army, which had only 2,116 officers and 25,706 enlisted men. A partially-trained militia provided a 100,000 man reserve. As in the past, the government counted on civilian volunteers to fill the ranks.

Benign Secretary of War Russell Alger ran his moth-eaten military establishment on a miserly congressional handout. The troops carried old-fashioned Civil-War type Springfield rifles—cumbersome weapons that fired black powder cartridges and were practically useless in combat. The Danish-made Krag-Jorgenson rifle, a modern, bolt-action breech-loader, had been doled out to some regular army units. On the whole the U.S. Army was equipped for little more than chasing Indians.

Premier Sagasta knew he had not much to fear from the American army. But he also knew that the time was rapidly approaching when technical skill, not numbers would decide a war. The Franco-Prussian conflict of 1870-71 had proven that.

Spain was an agricultural, semifeudal nation where illiteracy ran almost 60%; the U.S. was highly industrialized and literate. Mechanical ability seemed an almost universal American talent; machinery was a mystery to most Spaniards. The intricacies of a machine gun, for insatnce, presented no problem to the average American soldier, but in the Spanish Army only a few hand-picked men, usually officers, could

National Guardsmen mustered into Federal service swear loyalty to the U.S. (top). An infantry company in full marching gear awaits orders to start out on a hike at undesignated training camp (center). Officer holds kit inspection in company street, a ritual familiar to veterans of any war (bottom).

fathom the workings of the gun.

For such reasons Sagasta swallowed his pride and told Woodford, "My government will abide by any decision of an international commission regarding the *Maine* . . ." He also proposed an armistice in Cuba (with or without *insurrecto* consent) and outlined a liberal program for the island which virtually guaranteed freedom within a reasonable, but unspecified, time.

Sagasta's conciliatory terms led Woodford to cable McKinley on April 9: "I hope nothing will be done now to humiliate Spain . . . I am satisfied . . . Sagasta means to have peace . . ."

McKinley read Woodford's message without joy. The Ambassador's despatch virtually guaranteed that there would be no war. But much had happened to President McKinley since the *Maine* report was published.

Public pressure for war had mounted; the Yellow Press ran daily banner heads: *Remember The Maine!* Letters, telegrams and telephone calls demanding war bombarded the White House. Congressmen and Senators of McKinley's own Republican Party urged the President to call for a war vote.

The Chief Executive wrestled with his conscience. He spent sleepless nights seeking a solution that would satisfy everyone. According to a White House aide: "I thought the President was on the verge of a total breakdown . . ." In addition to the weighty problems of state which beset him, McKinley was also faced by personal tragedy. Mrs. McKinley's health had failed and she remained confined to her chambers, an almost total invalid.

The President was scheduled to speak before Congress on Wednesday, April 6, but had postponed his

Rookies of awkward squad learn mysteries of close order drill under officer's watchful eyes. Note man wearing civilian clothes.

talk until Monday, April 11, for a number of reasons: A delegation made up of diplomats from Germany, Austria-Hungary, France, Great Britain, Italy and Russia, was coming on the 7th, to find a formula for a peaceful settlement of the Spanish-American difficulties.

More important, Consul Fitzhugh Lee had requested at least five days to evacuate Americans from Cuba before the presidential message. Army and Navy officials had asked for more time to prepare the armed forces in the event of war.

McKinley came to a decision on what course to pursue when one of his most ardent supporters, Secretary of War Alger was told by a Republican Senator: "You'd better advise the President to ask for a declaration of war. If not, he's in danger of ruining himself and the Republican Party by standing in the way of the people's wishes . . . Congress will declare war in spite of him. He'll get run over and the party with him . . ."

Cavalry troopers ride out near Tampa, Florida.

A pack mule train, accompanied by cavalry, takes a practice march along a Florida road near Tampa.

A stronger executive than McKinley might have gone his own way, but he was no crusader, merely a politician trying to do the right thing and please everyone.

Senator Lodge warned him: "If the Republican Party does nothing about Cuba we shall go down to the greatest defeat ever known . . ." President McKinley was a loyal party man; he could not allow such a misfortune to befall the country. In his opinion, only Republicans could keep the U.S. economically sound and prosperous.

Even though McKinley detested war, he had deep sympathies for the struggling Cubans and favored their cause. Also, he had misgivings about Premier Sagasta and did not trust the Spaniard. Although Sagasta was an honorable man and a proven liberal, McKinley feared he was planning some shady "Latin" trick. Not even the President could quite rise above the rampant prejudices of the era in which he lived.

Convinced that war was justified, McKinley rebuffed the mixed delegation of European powers and refused to engage in any further negotiations on the Spanish crisis.

"The chronic disturbance in Cuba deeply injure the interests and menace the tranquility of the American nation by the character and consequences of the struggle thus kept up at our doors . . . besides shocking its sentiment of humanity. . ." McKinley told the delegates.

"We hope for humanity's sake that you will not go to war," one of the emissaries said.

"If we do, we hope you will understand that it is for humanity's sake," the President replied. "Let us also hope that under the Providence of God some way may yet be found to bring about peace without the resort to arms . . ."

Possibly McKinley felt some twing of conscience as he made this pious remark. American motives in Cuba were not based solely on humanitarian grounds: U.S. citizens had more than $50,000,000 invested in Cuban sugar plantations, iron mines and tobacco farms.

National trade with Cuba ran to over $100,000,000 annually. The island's unsettled conditions adversely affected this flow of business. It was quite likely that commercial and financial aspects of the situation far outweighed any humane ones in determining U.S. policy towards Cuba. . .

Scowling Uncle Sam takes a fighting stance alongside an idealized Cuban insurrecto in this editorial cartoon which appeared after declaration of war.

WAR–April 11, 1898

The first U.S. fighting arm to go on active duty was the Navy. Elements of the Atlantic Squadron are shown sailing towards Cuba.

On Monday, April 11, 1898, the U.S. Congress held a momentous joint session. The President's speech that day marked a turning point in American destiny. McKinley's words lifted the U.S. from its traditional isolationism and set the country on the road to colonialism, imperialism, participation in two world wars and a crucial role on the world stage.

Standing before a hushed, packed house, McKinley summarized the Cuban situation in a long speech which he concluded by saying:

"The only hope of relief and repose from a condition which can no longer be endured is the enforced pacification of Cuba . . .

In the name of humanity, in the name of civilization, in behalf of endangered American interests I ask Congress to authorize and empower the President to take measures to secure a full and final termination between Spain and Cuba . . . and to secure on that island . . . a government capable of maintaining order and insuring the security of its citizens as well as our own, and to use the military and naval forces of the United States as may be made necessary for these purposes . . ."

McKinley gave no ringing call to arms, but he had asked for intervention in Cuba, although a definite date was not mentioned. Congress soon filled that lack.

On Wednesday, April 20, both House and Senate voted an ultimatum demanding that Spain ". . . at once relinquish its authority and government in the island of Cuba and withdraw its land and naval forces from Cuba and Cuban waters . . ."

The American warning added that the President would wait until noon of Saturday, April 23, for a "full and satisfactory response," otherwise he would use "all the power of the United States" to enforce the ultimatum.

The U.S. terms were vehemently rejected by Spain. Premier Sagasta in a stirring plea called on "all sons of Spain . . . to repel with the whole might of the nation a most odious outrage . . ." Ambassador Woodford was handed his passport and the Spanish Ambassador at Washington asked for safe conduct; with the end of diplomatic relations between the two countries the last obstacle to war removed.

Woodford's departure from Spain was marred by violent anti-American demonstrations and riots which imperilled the Ambassador and his party. He finally boarded a ship at Barcelona and sailed for the U.S.

Once Woodford had cleared Spanish waters, Congress declared that a state of war had existed since Thursday, April 21. Appended to the war resolution was an amendment sponsored by Senator Henry Moore Teller of Colorado. The Teller Amendment forbade an American annexation of Cuba and said in part:

> ". . . The United States disclaims any . . . jurisdiction or control over Cuba . . . Once hostilities are concluded we will leave the government and control of that island to its people . . . Cubans are, and of a right ought to be, free and independent . . ."

Congressional expansionists did not like the amendment but Teller's rider passed without difficulty.

The U.S. faced a major war for the first time since 1865. By Friday, April 22, McKinley declared a blockade of all Cuban ports. That very day vessels of the Atlantic Squadron sortied from Key West to implement his orders.

The President was authorized by Congress, on April 23, to call up 125,000 volunteers for the duration of the war. Recruiting stations all over the country were swamped by eager young men, rushing to join the colors. They came from every walk of life: farmers, students, clerks, merchants, teachers and cowboys.

With searchlights sweeping the waters and signal rockets streaking skyward, U.S. naval units keep a tight blockade on the approaches to Havana.

(That same spring, the discovery of gold in the Klondike region of the Yukon Territory also offered a young man a different brand of adventure. The lure of gold was great, but most chose to join up and fight.)

The Yellow Press cartoonists depicted Uncle Sam with clenched fists, his sleeves rolled up, glowering off towards Cuba. "By Juniper!" said Uncle Sam, "I'll have peace if I have to fight for it!"

More than 60,000,000 Americans—with the exception of a few dissenters—jubilantly hailed the belated declaration of war. There was a fervor and enthusiasm which a Kansas editor described in this way:

> "In this glorious April, everywhere over our good, fair land flags are flying . . . Trains carrying soldiers roll to the Southland and little children sitting on fences along the way greet the soldiers with flapping scarfs and handkerchiefs and flags . . . at the stations, crowds gather to hurrah the soldiers and to throw hats in the air, and to unfurl flags . . ."

Not since '61 had the U.S. witnessed such stirring scenes. Petty hatreds were forgotten and even "greenhorns" felt they belonged; among the volunteers were thousands of recently arrived immigrants.

Negroes, so long the targets of bigots and racists, suddenly were treated with respect. (Unfortunately, this lasted only a brief time.) When the 10th Cavalry, a Negro unit of the regular army, entrained for a camp at Tampa, Florida, a *New York Sun* reporter wrote: ". . . what a fine body of a men are these dusky warriors . . . We salute our ebony-skinned heroes whose lustrous eyes gleam with martial fire. . ."

Few Americans took the enemy seriously.

Everyone knew the "dagos" couldn't fight! "Why, they don't stand a chance against us . . . They can't lick a bunch of half-starved Cubans . . . We'll make 'em howl!" a volunteer wrote his parents.

Patriotic fevor was contagious and outspoken anti-war partisans entered wholeheartedly into the crusade to free the Cubans. "*Cuba Libre!*" joined

"*Remember The Maine*"! as watchwords of the day.

Even William Jennings Bryan, who had been the Democratic candidate for president in 1896, and McKinley's prime opponent in that election, joined the army as a private when war was declared.

The 38-year-old Nebraskan, known as the Great Commoner, had long advocated international peace. He explained his change of view, saying: ". . . Our country has embarked on a noble path . . . This is a moment when all men of good will must stand ready to fight and die if necessary!"

The War Department felt that since Bryan had been a presidential aspirant, it was not fitting for him to remain a buck private. He was quickly appointed colonel of the 3rd Nebraska Volunteers.

"Seldom was a man less qualified for a post," a newspaperman said. "With his ill-fitting uniform and long hair, Bryan looked like no soldier before or since."

Fortunately for the men of the 3rd Nebraska, Bryan never led them in combat and the regiment saw no frontline service; but other units were destined to fight soon enough.

Nobody seemed to care what lay ahead that hysterical April; seldom had a nation entered a war with such abandon and carefree ardor. Americans went to war with wide-eyed innocence. Perhaps it was better that they did not know what lay in store. Many youths would meet death from yellow fever, malaria measles, ptomaine poisoning, typhoid and dysentery; only a relative handful would die in battle. Germs caused more casualties than did Spanish bullets.

But all this was in the future.

That April the war was music, cheering and flags. No one had thoughts of pain or death. Teddy Roosevelt summed up the national outlook in a single word when he heard war had been declared.

"Bully!" Roosevelt cried.

And the country echoed: "Bully!" which in 1898 slang meant everything was wonderful.

It would be a bully war!

THE SPLENDID LITTLE WAR
April 1898-August 1898

Thanks to Secretary of the Navy Long and his bustling assistant, Teddy Roosevelt, every ship of the U.S. Navy was in fighting trim.

The powerful Atlantic Squadron commanded by Rear Admiral (formerly Captain) William T. Sampson proceeded at once to its blockade stations off Cuba. A mighty reinforcement was already *en route* to Sampson. Weeks before the actual declaration of war, Secretary Long had made an important move. The 10,288-ton battleship *Oregon*, launched at San Francisco in 1893, was needed to bolster the Atlantic Squadron, Long decided.

On March 6, the *Oregon* was in drydock at Bremerton, Washington. That day, her captain, Charles E. Clark, received orders to join Sampson at Key West, with all speed. This meant a hazardous 15,000-mile journey down the west coast of South America through the Strait of Magellan, and into the Atlantic.

Naval strategists for years had been urging the construction of a canal across the Isthmus of Panama or some other point in Central America to assure the rapid movement of ships from ocean to ocean.

The *Oregon's* voyage dramatized this need.

The battleship left Bremerton for San Francisco where she took on coal and supplies; by March 19, the vessel was plowing through the worst storm the South Atlantic had experienced in living memory. Despite foul weather, the *Oregon* reached Key West in 68 days, a record for the time.

The clamor for a Panama Canal grew stronger. Several attempts had been made to dig one, but each ended in failure, the most recent in 1888, when a French company's efforts came to a financially disastrous conclusion.

A leading newspaper editorial summed up the arguments of the canal's proponents: "Had such a waterway been in existence, the *Oregon's* hazardous journey would have been greatly lessened . . . We dare delay no longer the building of a canal linking the Atlantic and the Pacific. Our national safety demands that this project be launched at once!"

However, the Panama Canal was years away and the stark realities of war began to trouble Americans living in coastal cities on the Atlantic seaboard. Daily, fears grew that the Spanish fleet would swoop down and ravage New York, Boston, Baltimore, Philadelphia or New Orleans. Rumors flew of Spanish flotillas being sighted. Philadelphia was in near panic when word spread that six enemy cruisers were maneuvering outside the harbor. At the same hour, reports of Spanish

war vessels were heard from New York, New Orleans, Baltimore and Charleston, South Carolina.

A quick tally showed that the "ghost ships" numbered more than the entire strength of the Spanish Navy.

As days went by, coastal defenses were strengthened but anxiety still ran high. Shippers fretted about the safety of cargo vessels still at sea. A high New York official worried that enemy ships would steam through the Narrows and bombard the metropolis.

All these fears were groundless. The Spanish Navy could carry out no raids; its ships were in disrepair; several cruisers had defective guns; turrets were scarred and pitted with rust.

The commander of the Spanish Navy, Admiral Pascual Cervera y Topete, well knew the wretched condition of his fleet. When ordered to sail from Cadiz, Spain to the Canary Islands and then to Cuba, the Admiral dolefully wrote Premier Sagasta:

> ". . . Nothing can be expected for this expedition except the total destruction of the fleet . . . I deem it expedient that you should know . . . that while we are ready to meet honorable death in the line of duty . . . I think it certain the sacrifice of these naval forces will be as sure as it is fruitless and useless . . . I shudder for my poor Spain . . ."

Having expressed his personal feelings, Cervera left the Canaries and made for Cuba. In a skillfully conducted roundabout voyage, the Admiral brought his dilapidated ships to Santiago, Cuba. The Americans found the enemy fleet there after a frantic search and tightened the blockade on the port. A "flying squadron" of fast cruisers under Commodore Winfield Scott Schley, in the flagship *Brooklyn*, kept a steady vigil to bottle up Cervera.

The war's first shooting action took place on April 27 when the U.S.S. *Cincinnati*, a cruiser, accompanied by the monitor *Puritan*, opened fire on Matanzas Harbor at a distance of 5,000 yards. Rear Admiral Sampson's flagship, the armored cruiser *New York*, joined in the bombardment. The Americans pounded Spanish shore positions with some 300 shells of various calibre; the bombardment was highly ineffectual.

According to Spanish sources, the *Yanquis* (Yankees) used up all that ammunition to kill "one old mule." This aroused great hilarity in Havana and Madrid. The news of the inept bombardment mortified Admiral Sampson, the Navy Department and the nation . . .

One of the war's first heroes was Lieutenant Andrew S. Rowan, (top) who trekked across Cuba (map) to make contact with the Cuban guerilla leader Callixto Garcia. Rowan's feat was subject of inspirational pamphlet by Elbert Hubbard.

Muleteers prepare pack animals for a march. Note that mule-skinners are wearing civilian clothes. These men were hired by army in non-military capacity to handle pack mules.

In the opening phases of the war, the newspapers amplified every minor incident as though it had earth-shaking consequences. Thus, Army Lieutenant Andrew S. Rowan received undue publicity for going ashore on an isolated Cuban beach and stumbling through the jungles until he found the *insurrecto* leader Calixto Garcia. Rowan told him that the U.S. soon would back his fight with supplies, arms and ammunition.

The feat brought Rowan immortality when it was made the subject of a widely read pamphlet by Elbert Hubbard entitled, *A Message to Garcia*. Hubbard emphasized loyalty, enterprise and initiative in the face of obstacles and several generations of young Americans were bored and burdened by the contents of Hubbard's eulogy to Rowan.

In addition to creating heroes, the press spent much space speculating on an impending seaborne invasion of Cuba by the U.S. Army.

Command of that operation had fallen to General William Shafter who weighed nearly 300 pounds and suffered from chronic gout. Because of his physical condition, Shafter seemed singularly unsuited for tropical service. However, he was a brave, honest soldier, with an excellent Civil War record and long experience in fighting Indians. Secretary of War Alger knew and trusted the 63-year-old general who hailed from his home state of Michigan.

The Cuban invasion was hindered from the outset by Shafter's superior, General Nelson Appleton Miles, the Army's highest ranking officer. A vain and arrogant man, dubbed "The Peacock" by Teddy Roosevelt, Miles interfered with everything Shafter was doing to train and outfit a 25,000-man force at Tampa, Florida. Much time was wasted as Miles bickered with both Shafter and Alger.

A problem even more irksome than personality differences beset the Army. After more than three decades of incompetence and neglect, the War Department suddenly had to equip some 250,000 volunteers. (McKinley's initial call for 125,000 was soon increased by a similar number.)

Among the first to join the colors was Teddy Roosevelt who resigned as Assistant Secretary of the Navy to enlist in the First Volunteer Cavalry, which won fame as "The Rough Riders." Commissioned a lieutenant colonel, Roosevelt was executive officer to Colonel Leonard Wood, who commanded the Rough Riders.

The regiment, which assembled at San Antonio, Texas, was made up of cowboys, college athletes and hand-picked horsemen.

Unlike other volunteer units, the Rough Riders was well armed and disciplined, possibly one of the finest volunteer outfits ever mobilized. However, the regiment never received cavalry mounts and only the officers had horses. Although known by its catchy nickname the outfit was to fight on foot as infantry.

Most of the rapidly growing Army was far below Rough Rider standards. Officers and men lacked military experience; many of the volunteers, though eager and willing, could not tell a rifle's butt from the muzzle. National Guard and militia units could keep in step for an Independence Day parade, but that martial skill scarcely qualified them for combat in Cuba's jungles and mountains.

Gun commander signals halt as light field artillery crew runs through drill at Port Tampa, Florida, the army's main concentration point for the Cuban campaign.

Lieutenant Colonel Theodore "Teddy" Roosevelt, poses with his famed "Rough Riders", hand-picked horsemen who made up crack volunteer outfit. Ironically, the "Rough Riders" went into combat dismounted.

To cap the Army's many troubles, there was a shortage of everything the troops needed. The arsenals had no modern smokeless powder and the only uniforms available were of heavy blue woolen cloth far better for Alaska than Cuba. Blankets, cots, leggings, cartridge belts, knapsacks, tents, hats, shoes, canteens—all manner of material an army needed was in short supply.

But guardsmen, militiamen and volunteers, clad in blue woolens, streamed into training camps at Chickamauga, Georgia; Falls Church, Virginia; Mobile, Alabama; Tampa, Florida; and San Francisco, California.

Inexpertly set up and with inadequate sanitary facilities, the camps soon were rife with disease. Typhoid broke out in some of them and a measles epidemic laid low thousands. Spring rains made bogs of badly chosen bivouac sites. Hundreds were felled by scarlet fever, pneumonia, influenza and bronchitis. Understaffed and inefficiently operated, the Medical Corps could not cope with the situation. Young volunteers died by the score miles from the enemy; their stab at glory ended in a mudhole training camp.

From the first, the troops complained bitterly about the food. Someone raised the cry that the "boys" were being fed putrid meat. The soldiers called it "embalmed beef" and a standing army joke was: "We don't use cooks, we use undertakers to handle that stuff."

Thousands suffered food poisoning and dysentry was widespread. A major scandal brewed as Congress started to investigate the "embalmed" beef charges.

Somehow, in spite of the bungling, a sort of order evolved. Troops began training schedules as sanitary conditions were improved. Regular Army non-coms taught awkward farm boys the manual of arms Cavalry volunteers learned to handle horse, saber, revolver and carbine. Target practice was held. Miraculously, an army took shape.

Rumors about the impending Cuban invasion grew stronger; and signs of it were evident. General Shafter's Vth Corps, which would carry out the mission, established headquarters at Tampa. Troops arrived there daily. Officers gathered each evening on the porch of the Tampa Bay Hotel to talk over the coming campaign.

They were an oddly assorted group, according to Richard Harding Davis. He wrote in the *New York Journal*: "One could find at Tampa West Point classmates long resigned from the army . . . There were present men who had fought against each other and on the same side in the Civil War . . . They were no longer young, these balding, gray-haired, paunchy men . . . but in their eyes still flickered the steely glint of the warriors they once had been . . ."

Left to right Major General Nelson A. Miles, Commander-in-Chief of the U.S. Army. Major General William R. Shafter, commanding U.S. forces for the invasion of Cuba. Brigadier General Leonard Wood, commanding the "Rough Riders".

10,000 MILES AWAY

American eyes were fixed on Cuba, but the war's first major clash took place 10,000 miles away at Manila Bay in the revolt-torn Philippines. Few Americans, including government officials, knew anything about the Islands or the people who lived on them. Yet Filipinos had been intermittently fighting for freedom from Spain since the 16th Century when Ferdinand Magellan had claimed the Islands for the Spanish Crown.

In 1898 only 1,000 of the 7,803 islands making up the Philippine archipelago were inhabited. The bulk of the 10,000,000 Filipinos was on the two largest islands—Luzon and Mindanao, an area comparable to Illinois and Indiana. The Islanders belonged to many tribes and spoke 87 different dialects including Tagalog, Visayan, Bikol, Pampango and Pangasinan. Educated Filipinos were literate in Spanish.

The religion in Luzon was Christian, but in Mindanao, Samar, Zamboanga and other southern islands the people were Moslems of the fierce Moro tribe. While much Philippine territory was unexplored in the '90's, cultivated areas bore rich crops of rice, sugar, hemp and spices. The land was worked by Filipinos who were in virtual bondage to their Spanish masters.

The political, cultural and commercial center of the Philippines was the capital, Manila, which had a population of 300,000. Most of the city's populace lived in the direst poverty; men, women and children worked at the main industry—cigar making—under unsanitary and intolerable conditions.

Spaniards and other Europeans lived opulently in fine homes making a sharp contrast to the miserable existence of the natives. But the poverty that blighted Manila was mild when compared with that of the interior; in thousands of tiny jungle villages, Filipinos struggled to maintain themselves. The villages were clusters of straw huts raised on stilts to keep out floods and small animals.

Naked children played in mud and filth; diseases such as pellagra, yaws, trachoma, rickets, dengue fever, yellow fever and malaria were endemic. Rutted dirt wagon roads linked one village with another; sometimes a *cantina*, a church, a general store or a police station flanked the road.

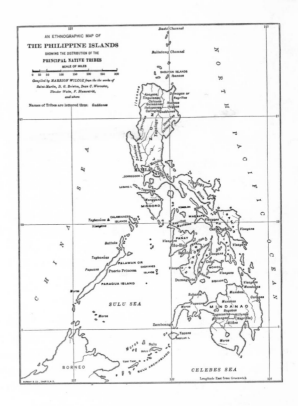

Map (top) of Philippine Islands. Typical natives of Luzon, center and bottom.

A view of the Escolta, the main thoroughfare of Manila, the main city in the Philippines.

Emilio Aguinaldo, leader of the Philippine insurrectos in their gallant struggle against Spain.

The jungle grew thickly on all sides. Monkeys chattered in tree tops, snakes slithered through the underbrush and gaily plumaged birds flitted through the tree tops. The jungle was filled with raucous bird-calls and deep silences; it was a mysterious and foreboding place.

Spain had done little to modernize her economically backward colony. The roads were abominable; transportation consisted of carts or wagon drawn by oxen. In all the Philippines there had been built only one single-track rail line which ran 120 miles from Manila to the Lingayen Gulf.

This was the land where a revolt erupted in August 1896, the latest of many uprisings that had occurred through the three-hundred-year-long Spanish reign. On Luzon, the most important island, a secret society called *Katipunan* conducted fierce guerilla warfare against their rulers.

One leader in this struggle was 27-year-old Emilio Aguinaldo. Short in stature—he stood only five-feet-four inches tall—Aguinaldo was deadly with sword and pistol. Of a middle-class background, the rebel chieftain was born March 22, 1869 in Kawit, Cavite Province, about 20 miles south of Manila, where he received a Catholic school education.

Intelligent, fervent and courageous, Aguinaldo and his *amigos*—which the *Katipunan* members called themselves—made life hellish for the Spaniards.

Amigos ambushed Spanish Army patrols and waylaid food convoys. They attacked outposts and burned supply dumps. Poorly armed, the Filipinos fought from behind rocks and trees; they launched swift hit-and-run assaults. Spanish sentries were decapitated by razor-sharp bolos.

The Spanish retaliated with great cruelty. They used Regular Army troops and Filipino mercenaries of the Maccabebe tribe to hunt down insurgents. (The *amigos* were mostly Tagalog tribesmen, the Maccabebe's traditional enemies.)

Filipinos resisted the Spanish in other than violent ways. Dr. Jose Rizal, a gentle, soft-spoken intellectual called upon the *amigos* to stop fighting.

"We can break the bonds of Spanish tyranny only through education! A literate people is a free people!" he cried.

As head of the *Liga Filipino* (Philippine League) Rizal presided over a group of native intelligentsia; bookish men, not men of action. Even though Rizal was against violence, the most warlike *amigo* respected him.

The gentle doctor presented no threat to Spain but when the revolution erupted in August 1896, Governor-General Camilio Polavieja, a brutal tyrant, arrested Dr. Rizal and sentenced him to death for treason. The sentence was caried out in Manila's beautiful Luneta Park before an audience of Spanish ladies and gentlemen who shouted "Olé!" as Rizal fell, riddled by bullets.

A Spanish official revealed why he had been executed. "Rizal was a traitor . . . he belonged to the aristocrat class, not with the lowly rabble! He had ideas, style, manners . . . he was a gentleman and so he had to die! Rizal was more dangerous to us than a hundred illiterate *amigos!*"

Poorly armed, raggedly dressed, these Filipinos
are typical of the troops who fought with Aguinaldo.

By mid-summer of 1896, more than 20,000 Tagalogs were massed around Cavite; another 10,000 *amigos* roved the mountains and jungles of Luzon and other islands. As the fighting raged, Emilio Aguinaldo emerged as both military and political head of the Independence movement. He showed himself to be a truly remarkable leader. Within a few months Aguinaldo set up a Revolutionary Congress, formed a provisional government and organized his untrained countrymen into skilled guerilla bands.

For two years *amigos* waged futile war against

Spanish might, without weapons or funds. Leaders, less capable than Aguinaldo, suffered crushing defeats at the hands of Spanish Regulars and their Maccabebe allies. By 1898, Queen Regent Maria Cristina of Spain, ruling for her twelve-year-old son Alfonso XIII, enmeshed in the Cuban revolution, could spare no more troops for the Philippines. She also saw that Polavieja's tyranny was unsuccessful. Wishing to end the Philippine revolt, the Queen replaced Polavieja with General Fernando Primo de Rivera, a soldier of a different breed. He was a topnotch field officer, and a shrewd diplomat.

Drawing by famed artist Howard Chandler Christy shows
Filipinos in action against Spanish. They rarely fought
in such organized fashion, preferring to use guerilla tactics.

Photograph taken moments before Spanish soldiers execute two Filipino prisoners. It was such cruelty which inspired the Filipinos to revolt.

Governor-General Camilio Polavieja, used brutal methods to suppress the natives. His barbarous treatment of the insurrectos failed to stem the insurrection.

De Rivera arranged a truce talk with Aguinaldo. He offered generous terms to conclude the long struggle. By now, even Aguinaldo had to admit that the *amigo* cause was doomed to defeat without additional arms and money.

The new Governor-General promised widespread reforms. Filipinos would be given equality with Spaniards; land would be distributed to all; freedom of speech and press was to be granted, plus Filipino representation in the Cortes at Madrid.

As a final inducement, De Rivera proposed reparations totalling $850,000 to be paid Aguinaldo and other *Katipunan* leaders if they would leave the islands. The Governor-General stressed that this was not to be construed as a bribe, but a token payment for all the Filipinos had been made to suffer.

After more discussion and consultation with his comrades, Aguinaldo agreed to accept De Rivera's proposals. The revolutionary leaders were to leave the Philippines for Hong Kong; upon their arrival, De Rivera promised to forward a draft of $400,000 drawn on a Hong Kong bank; the rest of the money would reach Hong Kong before February 28, 1898, in two installments.

Accompanied by 34 Katipunan leaders, Aguinaldo came out of the hills and sailed to Hong Kong. The revolution was declared over; celebrations rocked Manila and reverberated through the islands. De Rivera's bank draft was honored in Hong Kong and the ordeal of the Filipinos at last seemed over.

An uneasy peace settled over the Philippines; but before long, the *amigos* realized they had been tricked. The $450,000 balance due the Hong Kong exiles was never paid. De Rivera and other high Spanish officials divided up that tidy sum and lined their own pockets.

Even more upsetting to the islanders, De Rivera broke every term of the surrender agreement. The intolerable repression of the past was clamped down again especially on Luzon. De Rivera rounded-up known revolutionaries and ordered them shot. The Governor-General might have outsmarted the trusting Filipino peasants, but, in his arrogance, underestimated them.

Though unworldly, the natives had an overabundance of courage. Their best leaders a thousand miles away, lacking weapons, outraged Filipinos nevertheless rose against the Spanish once more. Guerilla bands again swooped out of the jungles ambushing, burning, raiding. Suddenly De Rivera had a full-scale war on his hands. Even heavily guarded Manila was not secure from *amigo* attacks.

Within sound of the city's churchbells, rebels attacked Spanish patrols. Each night Filipinos crept up on outposts, murdered the sentries and vanished, taking Spanish rifles and ammunition with them. As the revolt spread, Aguinaldo, in Hong Kong, feverishly sought to buy weapons for his countrymen. He went to Rounceville Wildman, the U.S. Consul at Hong Kong and offered premium prices for Springfield rifles. Wildman, who sympathized with Aguinaldo, tried to arrange the sale but was sternly ordered by the State Department to drop such activities.

"The United States will neither aid nor abet rebellion against constituted authority," Secretary of State William R. Day declared.

When someone pointed out that the U.S. was openly siding with Cubans fighting against the very government the Filipinos opposed, a State Department official snorted, "Cuba's on our doorstep—but who ever heard of the Philippines?"

Emilio Aguinaldo, (center) poses for picture surrounded by his chief aides in the Kapitunan just before sailing for Hong Kong in accordance with agreement ending Filipino revolt. Spanish authorities did not live up to terms of the truce and in 1898, the rebellion flared up again.

BATTLE OF MANILA
May 1, 1898

Admiral George Dewey stands on bridge of flagship Olympia during Battle of Manila Bay as colors are raised

Among other American who knew nothing about the Philippine Islands was President William McKinley. When a reporter queried him on the situation in those remote Pacific islands, the President replied, "I can't tell you within five hundred miles where the Philippine Islands are located—and what's more, I don't care. They are of no concern to the United States . . ."

At the time, the Chief Executive did not know that he would soon be deeply concerned about the Philippines and their problems. Emilo Aguinaldo, still searching for arms, journeyed to Singapore where he intended to solicit help from either the British, German, Japanese or Russian consuls. He arrived in mid-April and after a week was about to give up; the only response to his appeals had been doors slammed in his face.

On April 21, Aguinaldo received an urgent call from E. Spencer Pratt, the American consul-general in Singapore. The Filipino leader, invited to a secret meeting, was told that the U.S. had gone to war against Spain. Pratt asked him to help America by returning to the Philippines and leading the revolt on Luzon.

"What are we to gain by aiding the *Americanos?*" Aguinaldo asked.

"Independence!" Pratt declared. "We have no ambitions in the Philippines! We entered this war solely for the purpose of freeing Cuba and are solemnly obliged to leave that island once the Spanish have been driven out. Believe me, we want nothing from you and your people. Fight beside us and you shall attain all your dreams!"

Pratt's words were music to Aguinaldo. The dream of a free and independent Philippine Republic seemed at hand; this time, with the active support of the U.S., the *amigos* could not fail. Soon, his countrymen who had knelt in the dust for centuries, would stand proudly erect, no longer Spanish-ruled serfs, but free men!

Aguinaldo agreed to lead the fight on Luzon. By April 25, he was aboard the British packet boat *Malacca* steaming for Hong Kong and a strategy meeting with Commodore Dewey which the commander of the U.S. Asiatic Squadron had requested.

However, while Aguinaldo was *en route*, Dewey received a cable from the Navy Department ordering him to the Philippine Islands where he must ". . . seek out, capture, or destroy enemy ships . . ."

By midday April 24, the U.S. Navy's Asiatic Squadron sailed from Hong Kong with battle flags flying and the band of the flagship *Olympia* playing martial airs. The Squadron—the cruisers *Olympia, Baltimore, Raleigh* and *Boston,* plus the light cruiser *Concord,* the gunboat *Petrel,* the fast cutter *Hugh McCulloch,* and two cargo ships, *Nasham* and *Zafiro*—put in at Mirs Bay, a land-locked harbor about 35 miles north of Hong Kong.

View of Luzon Island as seen from approaching American warships, prior to naval engagement

Dewey spent two days there preparing ships and men for a battle that was to change forever U.S. foreign policy and the nation's future.

Spars, chests, hatch covers and all wooden objects that might be splintered by shells were shifted to the cargo vessels. Gun crews sweated many hours to perfect their aiming, loading and firing. Every weapon was cleaned, oiled, checked and rechecked.

On Wednesday, April 27, Dewey said, "We're as ready as we'll ever be." At 1:00 P. M. that afternoon, the signal "All Ships Follow" was raised on the *Olympia's* mainmast. The flagship's band, assembled on the foredeck, blared "El Capitan March." The U.S. Asiatic Squadron moved gracefully into the swells of the China Sea on a course for the Philippines. As crewmen chanted "Remember the Maine!" the strains of band music faded across the heaving waters.

While the American ships were sailing towards Manila, the creaky Spanish Asiatic Fleet rode at anchor in Manila Bay. The ten-mile-wide entrance to the bay could have been made into a death trap for any hostile naval force.

The channel was broken into narrow passageways by the high rocky islands of El Fraile, Corregidor and Caballo. Batteries emplaced on the three strongholds were situated to blast a ship out of the water. Properly placed mines and torpedos across the channel mouths could have blocked enemy craft.

But Admiral Patricio Montojo, the Spanish commander, was more interested in fun and frolic than naval defenses and strategy. His attitude was understandable. The squadron he commanded was a sorry affair. The best ship in it was the flagship, *Reina Cristina*, a 3500 ton steel cruiser which mounted six 6-inchers and 14 smaller guns. Montojo's squadron also had six other craft, including three ancient wooden ships, of which one was a hulk that had to be towed.

Commodore Dewey had been advised by Filipinos in Hong Kong that the Spanish fleet at Manila was no match for him; but he worried about the mines, torpedos and shore batteries reportedly guarding the approaches to Manila Bay. He often mentioned his mis-

givings to Captain Charles Gridley, the *Olympia's* skipper. From Commodore to the lowest ranking seaman, the men of the U.S. Asiatic Squadron dreaded the moment they would have to test the enemy's defenses. The mine menace aroused a feeling of gloom which almost overwhelmed the Americans as the squadron neared its destination.

A gunner on the *Olympia* noted in his diary: "We are all down in the dumps . . . To come so far only to be blasted out of the water by a hidden mine . . . without seeing the enemy, isn't a pleasant prospect."

A day out of Manila, officers and men carried out their duties "as though preparing for their own funerals . . ." An additional worry put more wrinkles in Dewey's brow. One of his aides pointed out still another danger—the shore-based batteries on Manila's waterfront.

"We're really sticking our necks into the noose," the officer said. "Should we pass the mine fields unscathed and escape the guns of Corregidor, Caballo and El Fraile, Montojo may retire into the harbor, where his heavy shore guns can pound us to bits . . . I frankly fear the outcome of this mission . . ."

"As do I," Dewey agreed. "But I have my orders and will carry them out at all costs."

The Commodore and his men might have spared themselves such anxieties. No Spanish mines had been placed in the approaches to Manila Harbor until April 19 and those laid had faulty firing mechanisms. A string of torpedoes placed across the Caballo passage at the same time was also defective. Manila's shore batteries offered no danger to the Americans. Most guns were not even manned. The merchants and business men of the city had persuaded Admiral Montojo not to place his ships under the protection of the batteries because American counter-shelling could damage commercial property in Manila.

Montojo assured the businessmen that he would make sure they suffered no losses. When Dewey's ships

Admiral Patricio Montojo (left) commanded the decrepit Spanish fleet guarding Manila. His squadron consisted of the 3500 ton cruiser Reina Cristina, mounting six-inch guns and six obsolete vessels that included three ancient wooden ships. Governor-General Basilio Augustin y Davila (right) commanded Spain's army in the Philippines. Although beset by insurrectos, Augustin issued a ringing proclamation which called upon his men to fight to the end.

Artist J. C. Schell depicts various U. S. warships that made up the American Asiatic Squadron. Prominent in foreground is the USS Olympia (29), Dewey's hard-hitting flagship.

were sighted, the Admiral moved his flotilla to battle positions off Cavite in shallow water near Sangley Point.

When asked why he had chosen this area to make a stand, Montojo replied, "For the sake of our men. When the Americanos sink our ships, the masts will protrude out of the water. Our sailors can climb to the top and wait in safety until rescued, Otherwise everyone might drown."

Governor-General Basilio Augustin y Davila, who had replaced De Rivera, issued a stirring proclamation when told the Americans were on the way. "Let us resist with courage and the patriotic cry *Viva España!*"

Filipinos greeted his words with scorn. Aguinaldo had already told them the *Americanos* were coming as liberators. "Where you see the American flag flying, assemble in numbers," he urged. In their jungle hideouts, the *amigos* loaded rifles, sharpened bolos and bided their time.

At last, in the predawn hours of Sunday, May 1, the American ships appeared, creeping cautiously through calm waters, every man braced for the shattering roar of an exploding mine. Past Corregidor the fleet sneaked without being spotted by sentries; then, a signal flare streaked up from El Fraile, whose guns opened a noisy barrage. Shells bracketed the American warships but scored no hit. The cruisers *Raleigh* and *Boston* plus the gunboat *Concord* answered the enemy and silenced his guns.

Captain Charles Gridley, skipper of the Olympia **received Dewey's famous order, "You may fire when ready", to open the naval Battle of Manila at 4:00 A.M., Sunday, May 1, 1898.**

Bird's eye view of port facilities at Cavite shows shed, arsenal, fortifications. Note sunken Spanish ship in channel and U. S. fleet (background) after naval engagement.

Blazing action at height of Battle of Manila is depicted in this drawing. U.S. flagship Olympia is seen (center) firing at burning Spanish flagship Reina Cristina (right).

Commodore Dewey, on the *Olympia's* bridge, sipped cold tea "to settle his stomach" and issued a string of orders that kept his staff hopping back and forth. By 4:00 A.M., to the amazement of all aboard the American ships the entire squadron steamed unharmed into the broad waters of Manila Bay. Hardtack and coffee were served the men at battle stations; weary sailors wolfed the meager breakfast and snatched some sleep beside their cannon.

The Spanish fleet was sighted off Sangley Point shortly after daybreak. As the sun rose, the temperature soared and the heat became intolerable. The American sailors shed their shirts and awaited word to open fire.

Admiral Montojo's aged ships started the battle, their obsolete guns loosing broadsides at the Americans. The Spanish shells splashed into the water without finding a mark. At 5:41 A.M., Dewey, who had been observing the enemy through binoculars, turned to the *Olympia's* captain and said, "You may fire when ready, Gridley!"

Minutes later, the U.S. fleet's 6-inchers and 8-inchers were hammering away; when the smoke cleared, a resounding cheer went up from the Americans. The Spanish fleet was mortally wounded. Smoke and flame belched from the *Reina Cristina;* the other vessels were either driven aground, afire or sinking. By mid-morning the battle was over—a total disaster for the Spanish who lost 381 killed and wounded. Dewey's casualties numbered only eight wounded and one dead. There never before had been such a lopsided victory in the history of modern naval warfare.

From time to time, a shore battery guarding Manila Harbor blasted away at the Americans. When Montojo's resistance ended, Dewey swung his guns towards the city and warned Governor General Augustin y Davila that he would bombard Manila unless the shore batteries ceased fire. He also demanded he right to put ashore a party under a truce flag and send a message over the Manila-Hong Kong cable.

Augustin y Davila ordered the guns to be silenced but refused permission for Dewey to use the cable. "This city is not in *Yanqui* hands! No *Yanqui* will set foot here without a fight! I refuse unconditionally to give my consent . . ."

Angered because the cable had been denied him, Dewey had it hauled up and cut in half, thus severing Manila's only modern communications link with the outside world. This peevish act proved more irksome to the choleric American than to the enemy.

Augustin y Davila had no desire to let the world know of Montojo's defeat, but Dewey was anxious for the news to get out. His quick temper, which earned him many enemies in the Navy Department, had boomeranged. He was the victim of his own rashness; above all, Dewey wanted glory, and through his own act, had to wait for the praise he had earned.

Instead of bemoaning his error, Dewey consolidated his gains. On May 2nd and 3rd, he sent landing parties ashore at Cavite and seized the well-stocked arsenal there without resistance. At the same time American bluejackets occupied the villages of Cavite and San Roque. But even before the U.S. sailors landed, bands of *amigos* looted the arsenal and took away many Mauser rifles and ammunition for them.

The rebels had seen the Stars and Stripes flying and were rallying to the *Yanquis.* "With the *Americanos* to help us, we shall drive the last Spaniard from the Philippines! Filipinos! The hour is at hand! Strike a blow for freedom!" an *amigo* leaflet urged.

Once he had secured Cavite, Dewey sent the *Raleigh* and the *Baltimore* to Corregidor where the garrison there meekly surrendered. El Fraile and Caballo also raised the white flag. On Saturday, May 7, the Commodore dispatched the cutter *McCulloch* to Hong Kong. Her skipper had orders to cable Washington about recent events. He was also instructed to bring Aguinaldo to Cavite where Dewey had set up temporary headquarters.

The *McCulloch* reached Hong Kong Monday, May 9. In Dewey's name, her captain cabled:

> "On May 1, the squadron met and vanquished the enemy . . . I have taken possession of the naval station at Cavite, Philippine Islands . . . I control Manila Bay completely and can take the city at any time . . . but have not sufficient men to hold it . . ."

The news of Dewey's victory brought jubilation to the American people. Secretary of The Navy Long immediately promoted the Commodore to Rear Admiral, but that did not satisfy Congress which created a rank —Admiral of the Navy—especially for the new national hero.

William Randolph Hearst crowed: "How do you like the *Journal's* war?"

Apparently the eager thousands who rushed to buy his newspaper liked it very much.

Forward 6-inch gun turret of the USS Olympia in action against the Spanish ships (right). Other warships of U.S. squadron are seen deploying in firing position (left).

The destruction of the Spanish fleet with so few American losses started what amounted to a religious revival in the U.S. Crowds flocked to churches and synagogues; grateful worshippers gave thanks for the victory.

But whether Divine intercession or poor Spanish markmanship brought about the overwhelming American triumph had little bearing. The presence of the U.S. Asiatic Squadron in Manila Bay gave the administration a fresh dilemma. What was to be done about the Philippines? "The captured islands," a high official called them.

One American diplomat, John Barrett, the Minister of Siam, told a newsman, "It is of the greatest importance that the United States should take the Philippine Islands. Their value is not realized at home. They are richer and far larger than Cuba, and in the hands of a strong power would be the key to the Far East . . ."

Dewey's victory had opened a door to new territory and expansionists in the U.S. did not intend to let it slam shut. The nation had committed itself to a policy of independence for Cuba, but only an unofficial promise to Aguinaldo hobbled the imperialists' ambitions for the Philippines.

Filipino insurrectionists began having vague misgivings about the *Americanos*. Apolinario Mabini, one of Aguinaldo's top aides, wrote a memorandum to his chief just before the latter sailed from Hong Kong on the *McCulloch*. According to Mabini, the U.S. had entered the war only to protect its business interests in Cuba. He predicted that America would win the conflict and demand the Philippines as indemnity. "Let us be logical," he wrote. "Americans, like Spaniards, as well as all European nations covet this very beautiful pearl of the Oriental sea . . ."

Aguinaldo was troubled as he paced the deck of the *McCulloch;* the suggestion that he and his *amigos* might have to fight the Americanos upset him. Yet, he respected Mabini's opinions and resolved to watch his *Yanqui* allies with caution.

Back in the U.S., General Wesley Merritt, the second ranking officer of the Army, had been ordered to San Francisco where the VIIIth Corps was being formed for duty in the Philippines under his command. Merritt's orders read that he was to rout the Spanish, establish order and enforce U.S. sovereignty. But in so doing, he was to assure the Filipinos that the U.S. wished only to protect, not fight them.

The orders puzzled Merritt. He asked President McKinley, "Am I to seize the entire Philippines Archipelago or only Manila?"

To this the President replied: "all the islands will be given order and security while in the possession of the United States . . ."

The situation in the Philippines remained cloudy for weeks. No one could foretell what was going to happen when Aguinaldo returned to his homeland. On May 19, the *McCulloch* dropped anchor in Manila Bay. A launch sped from the *Olympia* to pick up Aguinaldo and his lieutenants. Aboard the cruiser, the *amigo* leader was met by Admiral Dewey, who greeted him with a hearty handclasp and some promises which led to much trouble in the future.

When Aguinaldo left the conference he had the Admiral's assurance that the U.S. would grant the Filipinos self-government once Spain was whipped. For many decades, controversy raged over what actually had been guaranteed. Apparently Dewey had given Aguinaldo assurances that independence for the islands was a certainty.

"But that is in the future. The task now is not to form a Philippine government but to defeat the common foe. Go ashore, start your army and together we'll smash the Spanish," Dewey allegedly told Aguinaldo.

Filipino insurgents spring an ambush on Spanish troops jungle somewhere near Manila. Insurrectos were adept at this type of fighting which caused heavy casualties to Spaniards.

The Admiral even suggested that a Philippine national flag be designed. "However, don't unfurl it until the moment is right," he advised.

The men parted amicably. Aguinaldo went ashore and the news of his arrival brought unrestrained joy to Luzon. Thousands of volunteers rushed to Cavite, begging for weapons; 12,000 Filipino militiamen attached to the Spanish Army deserted and came over to Aguinaldo with their arms.

The Americans watched in amazement as barefoot natives formed into a disciplined army—marching, drilling and handling their Mausers with admirable deftness. Even the most cynical *Yanqui* had to admit that the 'gugus' mean business . . ." (Gugu was a disparaging term by which some Americans called Filipinos.)

Affairs moved quickly. Aguinaldo wasted no time in setting up the framework of an independent country. He proclaimed himself president of the "Philippine War Government," issuing a statement which declared: ". . . we Filipinos are competent to govern ourselves without help from anyone . . ."

On June 18, 1898, Aguinaldo announced the Philippine Declaration of Independence. "This is a day to be celebrated in perpetuity! The birthday of our republic . . . a glorious moment, a splendid hour!" he said.

Expectations ran high among the Filipinos. Surely now the *Americano Presidente* would give his blessings to the free government of the Philippines. Had not the great Admiral Dewey written: "In my opinion these people are superior in intelligence and more capable of self-government than he natives of Cuba and I am familiar with both races . . ."

But not even the Hero of Manila Bay could influence such men as Senator Henry Cabot Lodge who noted to a friend: ". . . the Philippines must be ours . . . We hold the other side of the Pacific and the value to this country is almost beyond imagination . . ."

Stormy days loomed for the islands.

There were dark clouds of Filipino mistrust about American plans for them. Although Dewey had told Aguinaldo to build an army, no word of friendship ever had come from Washington. The State Department acted as though the *amigos* did not even exist. Quite naturally Aguinaldo resented this treatment and determined to make the U.S. pay attention to him.

He openly flouted Dewey's advice and flew the new Philippine Republic flag. It flapped defiantly over fishing craft and other small boats in the harbor.

While Dewey awaited reinforcements, Aguinaldo loosed slashing attacks against key Spanish positions on Luzon. Before long he controlled most of the island. His 30,000-man army took dozens of strongpoints until only Manila remained to the enemy. But the capital was surrounded by swarms of *amigos* who dug 14 miles of entrenchments to bottle up the Spaniards. At the same time, revolutionary bands were busy everywhere, striking as far south as the Moro Islands.

Aguinaldo obviously had decided to seize all the territory he could before Americans arrived in force. With the Asiatic Squadron blockading Manila by sea and the insurgents by land, the 13,000 Spanish regulars in the city under General Fermin Jaudenes were in a hopeless trap. It was only a matter of time before the Spanish general must surrender—but to whom should he capitulate—Aguinaldo or the Americans?

Jaudenes refused to give up to "that rabble" as he called the *amigos*. He intended to hang on until the Americans came, although every day the insurgent noose was being drawn tighter. Dewey, who wanted Americans to take Manila, dispatched cables urging all speed in sending troops. (The line to Hong Kong had by that time been amended.)

The balance of power around Manila was soon to shift. On May 25, units of the VIIIth Corps, under General Thomas Anderson, sailed to the Philippines from San Francisco. Some 2500 regulars and volunteers

U.S. Naval landing Party has picture taken on rocky Wake Island, July 4, 1898. This isolated Pacific outpost became one of first U.S. land grabs in area.

Brigadier General Thomas Anderson of the VIII Corps commanded the first contingent of U.S. troops to leave the country for the Philippine Islands. His 2500 men set sail from San Francisco on May 25, 1898 and reached Manila on June 30. Anderson's men were soon heavily reinforced by the remainder of the VIII Corps.

tramped aboard three transports for the 10,000 mile journey.

It was the first armed expedition to travel that far by sea from the U.S. for the sole purpose of conquering and occupying foreign soil.

After a brief stop at Honolulu, the transports continued their voyage escorted by the cruiser U.S.S. *Charleston* which had been awaiting them at Pearl Harbor. Once at sea, Captain Henry Glass opened an envelope containing sealed orders and learned that the convoy's next port-of-call was Guam in the Marianas. He was ordered to "seize and claim Guam for the United States."

On June 20, the American ships hove to off Guam at the mouth of the harbor of San Luis D'Aspra. The *Charleston* fired 13 shells at the crumbling fort guarding the port. Glass then sent a boatload of U.S. Marines ashore. The Leathernecks raised the Stars and Stripes, rounded up the 60-man garrison and took them aboard one of the transports as prisoners. The first genuinely imperialistic act in U.S. history had been concluded without bloodshed. Guam now belonged to the U.S.

When news of the feat reached Washington, Senator Lodge gleefully remarked, "I cannot conceive why the President wanted Guam unless he intends to keep the Philippines. Alone, Guam is worthless. As an outpost for the Philippines it has incalculable value for this nation . . ."

Ten days later, the convoy reached Manila and anchored near Dewey's warships. Soldiers crowded the rails to stare at Luzon's lush green hills. Probably never before in modern military annals had troops—from their commander down—been in such total ignorance of the land they had come to invade. General Anderson, only lately a colonel in Alaska, admitted that he knew nothing about the Philippines, its people or politics.

"I couldn't tell a Filipino from a Hottentot," he said.

Anderson was a soldier, not a political science expert. The issues in the Philippines did not concern him. "We've been sent to fight and that's all we need to be told," he announced to his men.

The *Yanqui* soldiers began landing at Cavite on July 1. Aguinaldo watched the debarkation with some misgivings. "I knew the moment of truth was at hand," he wrote years later. "The *Americanos* were there either to free us or to enslave us. I was ready to greet them with an embrace or a bullet . . ."

Anderson's men were only the vanguard of the VIIIth Corps. Heavy reinforcements followed in their wake. On June 15, 3500 men under General Francis V. Greene departed from San Francisco; General Merritt and his staff set sail June 27 and two days later, General Arthur MacArthur left with 5000 troops.

Captain Henry Glass (left) of the U.S.S. Charleston.
The cruiser escorted convoy carrying Anderson. Glass had
sealed orders which sent him to Guam in the Marianas
Islands with instructions to "seize and claim" Guam
for the U.S.

Shore line of Guam looms in background as Charleston
fires salvo at crumbling Spanish fort guarding harbor
entrance (right). Straw covered huts and scantily-clad natives
are features of street in Guam village (right). Map (left)
shows the newly acquired U.S. possession captured June
20, 1898 after a bloodless landing.

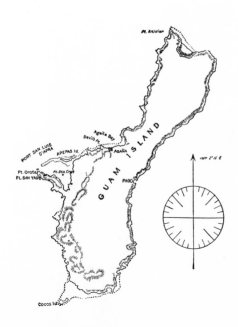

By the latter part of July, when the rainy season was at its height, some 12000 American soldiers had landed in the Philippines. It was becoming more evident each day that the Filipinos were growing resentful of the *Americanos* whose behavior towards the *amigos* was intolerable. Lumbering farmboys sneered at the small, dark-skinned natives they called "gugus."

As the strained relationship was stretched to the breaking point, Aguinaldo pointed out to both Dewey and Anderson that his army could easily capture Manila without their assistance. He asked why the *Americanos* had come in such numbers without his knowledge or consent. "Whether or not you like it, the Philippine Republic exists," Aguinaldo said. "My government and army control these islands.

The period of friendliness and co-operation between Americans and Filipinos was nearly at an end. Disputes over troop deployment and position boundaries were frequent; the insurgents arrested two U.S. officers for "entering their lines." Violence flared. A drunken U.S. regular beat up three Filipinos before he was subdued. In another incident, an American private, flourishing a pistol, ran through a Cavite street, threatening to shoot "a couple of gugus, just for the fun of it . . ."

Dewey was bothered by the way local affairs had deteriorated. He cabled Washington: "Situation critical. Spanish may surrender at any moment. Greatest problem will be how to deal with Aguinaldo . . . He has become aggressive and even threatening to our army . . ."

Men of Anderson's command splash ashore at Manila. Spanish-held buildings in background burn briskly as foe puts them to the torch before retreating.

Hobson's Mission

More astute men than those who ran the State Department might have heeded Dewey's words. But many Washington officials and the American people as a whole had little interest in the Philippines. The full attention of the country and its leaders was still focused on Cuba. Popular and official interest centered around Admiral Sampson's blockade of Santiago where the Atlantic Squadron was deployed in a semi-circle six miles from the harbor mouth. Every night searchlights illuminated the anchorage where the Spanish ships lay trapped.

Sampson vigilantly maintained the blockade, fearful that enemy cruisers might break loose to raid shipping or attack cities on the U. S. mainland. At the time, he did not know the deplorable condition of Cervera's fleet. The universal dread of hard-hitting, swift Spanish cruisers was almost obsessive with Americans.

No matter what the cost, Sampson vowed to keep Cervera cooped up inside Santiago Harbor. He hit upon a scheme to block the narrow exit by sinking the 5000-ton, 330-foot collier Merrimac across the harbor mouth to cork the channel and prevent any possible passage by enemy ships. (It never dawned upon Sampson that this would also hamper the entry of U.S. vessels.)

The ticklish mission was assigned to Lieutenant Richard Pearson Hobson, a naval engineer. Seven seamen volunteered to help him on the assignment.

Hobson rigged the collier with ten electrically fired

These six sailors were volunteers on one of war's most perilous missions, the blowing up of the collier Merrimac **to blockade ship channel at Santiago, Cuba.**

Handsome Lieutenant Richard P. Hobson led daring party in Merrimac **feat under orders from Admiral William Sampson (center) and Commodore William Scott Schley (bottom).**

Commodore Schley peers through his binoculars (right) as Hobson and his men set out on doomed *Merrimac*.

With flames licking at the sunken coal-ship, Hobsen and his companions cling to a life raft after setting off explosive charges. Shells from land batteries kick up spurts of water around them.

torpedoes individually controlled from different points on the ship. He planned to bring the *Merrimac* under the guns of the Morro, Santiago's main fort, swing the ship across the channel, and then open the seacocks and explode the torpedoes to scuttle her.

The volunteers would escape in a catamaran-type lifeboat towed by the *Merrimac*. It was a perilous assignment. Troops and shore batteries guarded Santiago Harbor. Machine guns and other rapid firing weapons were emplaced to sweep the waters and the chances seemed slim that Hobson and his men could get away after scuttling their clumsy collier.

The *Merrimac* began her hazardous trip at 3.30 A.M., June 2. A Spanish picket boat opened fire when she was 500 yards south of the Morro. The shore batteries blazed away and smashed the ship's steering apparatus. Just a few lengths from the spot chosen to sink her, the *Merrimac* went out of control.

Hobson ordered the seacocks opened and all the torpedoes detonated, but shell splinters had so damaged their firing mechanisms that only two charges went off. With the collier listing to port, Hobson and his men dived off and clung to the underside of the lifeboat which was riddled by bullets and shrapnel. The *Merrimac* finally went down, masts and smokestack jutting out of the water. But she merely obstructed the channel and did not block it as planned.

Spanish searchlights probed the harbor and many boats went out to hunt the daring *Yanquis*. Just after sunrise, Hobson hailed a passing enemy steam launch. Admiral Cervera, who was aboard, personally pulled the American officer out of the water and congratulated him on his bravery. In the afternoon the Spanish Admiral sent word to Sampson that the *Merrimac* volunteers were uninjured and had been taken prisoners of war.

Action at Guantanamo Bay

In first land action on Cuban soil, U.S. Marines keep up brisk fire on fleeing Spaniards at Guantamano Bay. Leathernecks, commanded by Lieutenant Colonel Robert Huntington came from cruiser Marblehead.

The failure of the blockage forced Sampson to take more direct action. One June 6, the Atlantic Squadron bombarded Santiago with the heaviest naval barrage ever unleashed; however, the results were disappointing and little damage was done.

Realizing that the blockade might drag on indefinitely, Sampson decided to establish a coaling station at Guantanamo Bay, about 35 miles east of Santiago. The cruiser *Marblehead* commanded by Captain B.H. McCalla and the gunboat *Yankee* landed 100 Marines at Guantanamo after a brisk naval bombardment. The original landing force was strengthened by 600 additional Leathernecks under Lieutenant Colonel Robert W. Huntington. The Colonel set up a base which he named Camp McCalla for the *Marblehead's* skipper.

The first land action of the war in Cuba took place when the Spanish launched a three-day-long attack on Camp McCalla. The Leathernecks drove them off, counter-attacked, burned an enemy supply dump and blew up the only fresh-water well in Spanish possession. It was a fairly won victory but not without cost. Several Marines were killed and wounded.

Stephen Crane, the noted author of *The Red Badge of Courage* was the war correspondent for the *New York World*. He wrote a moving description of death in battle, the courage shown by the Leathernecks and his own fears as he felt "the hot hiss of the bullets trying to cut my hair."

Commander Bowman H. Mc Calla, skipper of the USS Marblehead brought Huntington's leathernecks to Guantamano. Marines established outpost called Camp Mc Calla to honor the cruiser's master.

U.S. Marines form skirmish line after landing at Guantamano Bay (below).

Chaos at Tampa

Battery E, 1st U.S. Field Artillery loading guns and equipment aboard freight cars for shipment to transport at Port Tampa, Florida prior to embarking on Cuban campaign.

The action at Camp McCalla was only a minor skirmish. The real fighting of the the Cuban campaign lay ahead. With Cervera entrapped at Santiago and Guantanamo Bay securely in American hands, the U.S. Army prepared to make its bow on the stage of war. General Shafter received orders to move the 25,000 men of his Vth Corps to Cuba beginning on May 26.

This caused incredible chaos in the small port of Tampa. Supplies and equipment started coming in, overtaxing the single track railway. Freight cars—only a few properly labelled to show their contents—were stalled for miles along the track. They carried guns, fodder, ammunition, clothing, harnesses and medicines all jumbled together. The stench of rotting bacon and spoiled meat tainted the air as provisions went bad under the Florida sun.

The muddle grew worse every day. "Not in this world or the next shall I see the equal of the mess at Tampa," wrote a Chicago newsman. "I have seen sights at dock and railhead I believe unmatched except in some huge lunatic asylum . . ."

While the avalanche of supplies all but buried Tampa, thirty steamers crowded the narrow channel to the wharf which had room for only eight vessels at a time.

Matters were so confused that General Shafter went to Port Tampa pier and took personal charge of loading the ships. Sweating in the tropical heat, he reminded one buck private of ". . . an immense ball of tallow . . . which might melt away in a deep puddle . . ."

The General's size made him the target for many cruel jibes. Cartoonists pictured him as an elephant, a hippopotamus or a bursting balloon. His excessive weight prevented him from riding a horse and Shafter went about in a specially constructed buckboard braced with extra sturdy springs.

This, of course, also evoked unseemly humor. However, Regular Army and Navy officers held Shafter in high regard. A typical opinion of him was that expressed by Captain Frank E. Chadwick of the cruiser *New York* who thought him to be "a man of thorough courage, a strong will and much strength of character . . ."

War correspondents sit for group picture at Tampa. Richard Harding Davis is wearing white tropical helmet. Author Stephen Crane is man in white suit (right).

Wagons of supplies are unloaded at rail siding near Tampa as army prepares to sail for Cuba.

Troops crowd Tampa docks while boarding transports on first leg of journey to Cuba.

Although the loading was mismanaged, Shafter announced on June 7 that embarkation would start the following day. This created an even greater hodge-podge than the cargo handling. A rumor spread that the transports could carry only 18,000 men—which would leave 7,000 stranded at Tampa.

Regimental commanders rushed madly to make sure their units were not going to be left on the beach. Soldiers raced to strike tents and break camp. By sunrise, June 8, a dozen regiments were streaming toward the port, the men sweating in heavy blue woolens, bent under 60-pound full field packs, three days' rations, rifles, canteens and cartridge belts filled with 125 rounds of ammunition.

Somehow, by mid-morning all troops were aboard ship. The biggest military expedition ever to leave the U.S. was ready to sail. For once, the rumors were correct, although they had over-estimated the capacity of the transports. Instead of 25,000 troops, only 15,058 enlisted men, 819 officers, 30 civilian clerks, 22 teamsters and packers and 107 stevedores were crammed aboard the vessels with 2,295 horses, 144 six-mule army wagons and 81 supply wagons.

The men were poorly equipped for tropical service. Several Regular Army units, fresh from duty in the Dakotas and Montana, still wore winter issue uniforms and besides fur-lined sleeping bags, also carried heavy overcoats.

At 2:00 P.M., June 8, the leading transports weighed anchor and, with whistles shrilling, slipped out into Tampa Bay. Thousands of men hung over the railings and climbed the rigging to wave farewell. From the pier, still cluttered with crates, cases and boxes, a band serenaded the departing troops with such popular tunes as "A Hot Time in the Old Town" and "Ta-ra-ra-boom-de-ay."

If General Shafter, aboard the headquarters ship *Seguranca*, expected smooth sailing, he suffered disappointment. His ship was about to pull out when a messenger rushed aboard with a telegram from Secretary of War Alger.

"*Await further orders from me before you sail*," the message read.

"Signal the transports to drop anchor," Shafter sighed. "We're not leaving yet!"

Soldiers of the 71st New York National Guard cheerfully await departure of train carrying them to troop ships at the Tampa piers.

Convoy of transports, supply vessels and freighters carrying combat troops sail out to sea escorted by a cruiser.

Alger's dispatch was based on a report by the patrol boat U.S.S. *Eagle* which claimed to have sighted two Spanish cruisers and two torpedo boats in the waters between Key West and Cuba. U.S. naval units spent five days hunting these vessels while the Vth Corps sweltered aboard the stifling transports.

Conditions on the ship became unbearable. According to one soldier, "It was a frightful ordeal . . . Under the hot sun men lay gasping for air below decks in foul holds . . . An outbreak of fever was feared . . . and we prayed there would be no typhus epidemic . . ."

During a brief visit ashore, Lieutenant Colonel Roosevelt cried in outrage to newspapermen: ". . . the soldiers are jammed together like animals on those fetid troop ships. We are in a sewer . . . a festering canal . . . stinking of rot and putrefaction . . ."

Discomforts and rigors were forgotten on June 14 when everyone was convinced that no Spanish flotilla roved the high seas and the convoy was permitted to proceed.

The transports reached Cuba on June 17 and circled aimlessly for three days until the ships dropped anchor off Santiago near the blockading fleet. Admiral Sampson boarded the *Seguranca* which then sailed to a point 18 miles west of Santiago where Shafter and Sampson, accompanied by their staff officers, landed to hold a meeting with Calixto Garcia, the *insurrecto* leader to whom Lieutenant Rowan had delivered the famed message.

A welcoming committee of ragged, bearded *insurrectos* carrying assorted weapons greeted the Americans of the palm-fringed beach. Garcia, a burly man with a flowing white mustache and professional goatee, made a flowery speech of welcome and then got down to business in a palm-fronded hut about a mile inland.

Ships of the U.S. Atlantic Squadron, commanded by Admiral William Sampson, bombard the Cuban coast to soften up defenses prior to troop landings.

Combat: Daiquiri and Siboney

While transports lay off shore, troops of General William Shafter's army are ferried into the beach at Daiquiri, Cuba, to mark initial U.S. landing on that war-torn island.

On the spot photograph catches American soldiers trudging to shore along the Daiquiri pier. The movement was unopposed by the Spaniards who had retreated to positions inland after naval bombardment.

It was decided that the American forces should land at Daiquiri and Siboney, some 15 miles east of Santiago to secure bases for an assault on Santiago. The invasion was scheduled for daybreak, Wednesday, June 22. The attacking troops were to be elements of General Joseph Wheeler's dismounted cavalry division and the Second Infantry Division, General Henry W. Lawton commanding.

Richard Harding Davis described the Daiquiri landing in these words: "God takes care of drunkards, sailors and the United States . . ." By the lowest military standards it was a miserable exhibition of ineptness, poor planning and outright stupidity. Had the Spaniards put up even mild resistance the Americans either would have been driven into the sea or else annihilated on the sands.

Lieutenant General Arsenio Linares, the Spanish commander, had 12,000 first-rate troops for the defense of Santiago at his disposal. Had he chosen to make a stand on the limestone cliffs that overlooked Daiquiri and Siboney, he could have inflicted tremendous losses on the invaders. Instead, his soldiers blew up a few installations and retreated to Santiago.

Shafter's troops landed under the cover of a barrage by the Atlantic Squadron. The big guns pounded jungle, hillside and beach without receiving a shot in return. When the bombardment ended a lone Cuban appeared waving a white flag.

"*Yanquis!* Come on! The Spanish have gone!" he cried in English.

More Cubans appeared to urge on the Americans. Swarms of small boats sped shoreward. The soldiers spilled ashore and raced inland.

Pack mules and officers' mounts were thrown off the transports and left to swim to the beach. Cavalry horses, dumped overboard from one ship, began swimming out to sea. A quick-witted bugler on land blew "Assembly," and the trained steeds wheeled about and splashed to him.

The poorly handled landing went on all afternoon. The beach soon became a welter of piled-up supplies. Fieldpieces were buried under cookstoves; needed ammunition was covered by cases of rations; everything was confusion and chaos.

American soldiers strolled aimlessly about fraternizing with the *insurrectos* who came out of the jungles to gaze rapturously at the tall *Yanquis.* In the first flush of goodwill, Cubans and Americans greeted each other warmly. "*Viva Cuba Libre!*" cried Shafter's troops. "*Vivan los Americanos!*" shouted the *insurrectos.*

However, after a few hours, the novelty of the meeting wore off. Americans resented sharing rations, tobacco and clothing with the dirty, unkempt jungle fighters.

"You couldn't turn around without some wheedling *insurrecto* begging something—even the clothes off your back . . . You couldn't shake 'em off . . . They'd just stand around, grinning and jabbering in their lingo . . . I got so the very sight of 'em made me sick," a young U.S. private recalled.

Cheering Cuban Rebels greet portly General William Shafter and Admiral William Sampson as their long boat touches Cuban soil near Daiquiri on June 20. American officers had come ashore to hold conference with insurrecto leader Callixto Garcia.

Cuban rebels such as these emaciated men were on the Daiquiri beaches to meet Shafter's troops when they arrived.

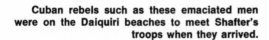

Although unsoldierly in bearing, the insurrectos (left) were capable of long marches through difficult terrain. Rebels shown here have come down from mountains to link up with Garcia at Daiquiri.

The glitter and tinsel of war soon rubbed off for the Americans. Back in the States, the *insurrectos* had seemed romantic and valiant warriors fighting for liberty; it was difficult to see them as half-naked scarecrows, crawling with lice and encrusted in filth. It seemed unbelievable that these bearded scavangers tearfully pleading for a cigarette could be the daring rebels who had captured the imagination and admiration of the American people.

"Why, they're like savages," exclaimed an officer from Boston.

He was unable to comprehend that men who had endured years of savagery could not be expected to observe the niceties of civilized behavior.

The *insurrectos* quickly sensed the contempt in which he *Americanos* held them. Despite this, they continued to cooperate in every way possible. Garcia's fighters guided the Americanos to Siboney and then slipped back into the jungle to harass the retreating Spaniards. The enemy's withdrawal ended at a village called La Guasimas, where Linares ordered his troops to entrench behind fortifications which guarded the road to Santiago.

Cuban reinforcements arrive by boat to bolster American troops who landed at Siboney, a few miles east of Santiago. U.S. soldiers came off transports and reached Siboney beach after nightfall in a clumsily handled operation.

As the Spaniards were digging in, more American troops came off the transports at Siboney. The new landings were made at night in utter disorder. The soldiers cavorted in the surf, laughing and splashing "like bathers at Coney Island on a hot Sunday," according to Richard Harding Davis.

The Spanish at Las Guasimas a few miles away heard the noise and must have wondered at the strange ways of the *Americanos*. They were to be even more astounded during the days and weeks that followed. No army had faced a more unorthodox foe; during the entire campaign the Americans flouted every military manual. Their only virtues as soldiers were brash courage and reckless ardor. It was a wholly inexperienced army. A few field grade and staff officers and some noncoms were Civil War veterans. Few regulars had ever been in a battle although some had fought Indians. Not one knew anything about fighting a disciplined foe armed with modern weapons.

This lack made little difference to the ranking officer ashore at Siboney. He was Major General Joseph Wheeler; three decades earlier he had been a hell-for-leather Confederate cavalry leader whose dash earned him the nickname "Fighting Joe." The years had whitened his hair and slowed his step but failed to dampen his martial ardor. Now in his sixties, the old soldier yearned for a last taste of glory.

General Shafter had remained aboard the *Seguranca* to supervise the unloading of supplies while the troops were landing at Siboney. This gave Wheeler a free hand on the beach. The aging warrior decided to attack the Spanish at Las Guasimas.

"It doesn't make sense to let the enemy hold a position which dominates our landing area," Wheeler told his staff. "So I've decided to kick him out of there."

Gray-bearded General Joseph Wheeler looked like a grandfatherly man but during the Civil War had earned the nickname "Fighting Joe" as a Confederate cavalry leader. Thirty years later he still was a fire-breathing warrior with the old Yankee foe.

Las Guasimas

Battlefield artist sketches American soldiers digging shallow entrenchments near Las Guasimas, shortly before the attack.

At dawn, June 24, without even informing Shafter, "Fighting Joe" sent the Rough Riders into battle supported by the Ist Cavalry and the 10th (Negro) Cavalry. A group of *insurrectos* also joined the assault on Las Guasimas.

The first American offensive of the war was conducted with vigor if not skill. After a brief, sharp skirmish, the Spaniards pulled out of their trenches and left Las Guasimas to the Americans. As the foe abandoned his lines, Wheeler jumped up and down, waving his sword and shouting, "Give 'em hell, lads! We've got the damn Yankees on the run!"

In the excitement he had confused his wars.

Wheeler won the fight at Las Guasimas at the cost of 16 dead and 52 wounded; despite the casualties, the troops profited from the experience—they had learned what it meant to be under fire.

General Shafter was dismayed when he heard about the battle. It had been his intention to use Lawton's regulars. Committing untested men into combat was risky business. However, Shafter could not complain too strenuously; Wheeler's dismounted cavalrymen had won a satisfactory victory. The capture of Las Guasimas was vital for a successful assault on Santiago.

The battle had some wholesome side effects. It raised the morale of all Shafter's troops and gave the folks back home something to cheer about. Newspaper correspondents created some new heroes; Colonel Leonard Wood and Lieutenant Colonel Teddy Roosevelt won glory, while the Rough Riders became the glamor boys of the Vth Corps and the darlings of all the American people.

Shafter praised Wheeler publicly but privately warned "Fighting Joe" not to fight any more battles without being ordered to do so.

After La Guasimas, engineers labored hard to improve the road that ran from that village to Siboney. The movement of supplies to the frontline troops went at a snail's pace over the twisting jungle wagon trail.

Supply ships were unloaded so slowly that the soldiers suffered a dearth of such essentials as rations and ammunition. These scarcities held up any further advance and the Army passed its time griping about conditions. A new worry furrowed Shafter's brows. The Caribbean hurricane season was at hand. Men scanned the skies for signs of an approaching storm. If foul weather scattered the supply ships, the troops at Las Guasimas, Siboney and Daiquiri would be in serious

An artillery battery moves out over wagon road
hacked through Cuban jungle on way to engage
Spaniards at Las Guasimas (above).

Spanish infantrymen trudge down main street
of village somewhere in Cuba (below).

difficulties.

General Shafter tried to expedite the landing of supplies and their transportation to the front. But the inexperienced cargo handlers bungled the job and the work proceeded slowly. Everyone worried about the weather, the slightest wisp of black cloud sent waves of apprehension through the men on ship and shore; every wind brought a hurricane alarm.

This concern was not limited to the Army in Cuba. McKinley and his cabinet held daily meetings to discuss the war situation. The weather in the Caribbean became the prime topic of discussion. U.S. government meteorologists were consulted about the possibilities of a hurricane striking at the time. The answer was far from reassuring.

"Due to the unpredictability of hurricanes . . . it must be assumed there is grave danger that such a phenomenon may occur . . . However, it is also likely that the region may remain unaffected . . ." a weather expert reported.

Anxiety for Shafter's men spread a trail of gloom across the country. There was much talk about weather and thousands crowded houses of worship to pray for fair skies over Cuba. Less reverent citizens placed bets on the date of the season's first hurricane.

About a week after the fighting at Las Guasimas, the cargo ships were almost completely unloaded. Guns, ammunition, ration, spare parts and medical supplies were safely on shore, stored under canvas. Best of all, the storms held off although it rained heavily at some time each day. But the hot sun came out after the downpours and dried up the ground so supply wagons and artillery caissons could keep rolling.

Wheeler's advance guard pushed on to El Pozo Hill beyond Siboney a point from which Fighting Joe reported that Santiago, seven or eight miles away could be plainly seen. He also noted that ". . . the hills about three miles to the south of the city from which Santiago can be shelled, appear deserted . . ."

The old war horse was wrong. Far from being deserted, those hills swarmed with Spaniards busily digging trenches and earthworks. General Linares had decided to make this high ground the main defense line of Santiago, wisely using the lull that followed Las Guasimas to strengthen his positions.

The Americans did nothing to stop him. Wheeler, overly cautious about avoiding another battle, did not even scout the enemy's positions. His men grumbled about the inactivity. They complained about the food, the rain, the heat and the lack of action. Morale ebbed dangerously low; the soldiers grew surly and insubordinate. As one trooper said, "We came to fight, not to sit around swatting mosquitos."

General Shafter was aware of the situation. Although suffering from malaria and almost crippled by gout, the corpulent general came up to El Pozo on June 30. He studied the Spanish entrenchments on San Juan Hill, Kettle Hill to the right of San Juan and the village of El Caney about four miles away. The enemy was observed barricading El Caney's streets and setting up gun positions on roof tops.

Shafter was convinced that an attack could be delayed no longer. *Insurrecto* scouts had reported that Spanish reinforcements were coming to Santiago from Manzanillo, 45 miles off. Garcia's men were harassing the relief force but could merely slow its progress, not halt it. Also, malaria was starting to take a toll of the Vth Corps and Shafter was concerned that jungle fever would cause more casualties than the foe's guns.

He ordered the attack for the next day, July 1. An infantry division supported by an artillery battery under General Lawton was to assault El Caney at dawn. Once the fighting there was under way, General J.F. Kent's 1st Division and the Dismounted Cavalry under General S.S. Sumner were to move against San Juan Hill and Kettle Hill. (Sumner, the senior brigade commander, had replaced Wheeler, who was stricken by fever.)

Weary American foot soldiers slog along rocky trail while heading for the fighting front during U.S. assault on Spanish positions around Las Guasimas.

Official map shows disposition of forces at battle of Las Guasimas, which was fought on Friday, June 24th, 1898.

San Juan and El Caney

Spirited charge by dismounted U.S. Cavalry regulars was turning point at battle of Las Guasimas. Artist Howard Chandler Christy captures fury of onslaught in this battlefield drawing.

Howard Chandler Christy.

from sketches made at
Las Guasimas, June

The initial stages of the attack began at 3:00 P.M. June 30, when Lawton, Kent and Summer moved their units to El Pozo in a driving rainstorm. The narrow roadway quickly became a quagmire of mud. Far to the rear hovered a Signal Corps balloon, towed by guy ropes which four enlisted men held. Riding in the balloon, high above the ground, was Colonel George Derby of the engineers.

By nightfall, the rain ended and a huge tropical moon hung in the clear, purple sky which was dotted with thousands of twinkling stars. The men slept on the ground and a soldier later wrote: ". . . before that moon would rise again, every sixth man who had slept in the mist that night would be either killed or wounded . . ."

With whips cracking, drivers shouting and horses straining, a light fieldpiece races up slope of El Pozo Hill to support front-line infantry.

The first target for Friday, July 1, was the village of El Caney, a hamlet of palm-thatched and tile-roofed buildings on a moderate hill. Its stone church dominated the village. Through the loop-holed wall, Spanish sharpshooters could fire at anyone approaching. About 500 yards south of El Caney stood a stone fort called El Viso, surrounded by trenches, barbed wire and supporting blockhouses. Linares held El Caney with about 600 men, against whom Shafter threw 6,000.

The U.S. artillery assigned to the attack on El Caney, San Juan Hill and Kettle Hill were obsolescent field guns. By 1898, the French 75 mm gun had been developed with its rapid fire mechanism and excellent aiming devices. But the U.S. Army was so backward in military science that no high War Department official had any concept of the tremendous advances made in the design of artillery.

At daybreak, July 1, the old guns began hammering away. Because American artillery fire was ineffectual, the fighting at El Caney, which Shafter had reckoned would last only a short time, raged on for hours. The village was finally taken in a heroic charge by the 25th (Negro) Infantry Regiment. The Americans lost 441 men at El Caney—81 killed and 360 wounded—while the enemy took casualties of 235 killed and wounded and 120 captured. The Spaniards had fought valiantly against ten-to-one odds.

As the struggle for El Caney went on, the assault on San Juan Hill and Kettle Hill got underway About 9:00 A.M. Kent's and Sumner's men moved down the slope of El Pozo Hill and entered the jungle. Some 10,000 troops advanced along a twisting trail hemmed in for most of its length by thick foliage, crossed by muddy streams and steaming under the heat of the sun.

The commanders knew little about their objective except that the enemy was strongly entrenched on the heights about a mile and a half away. In the first moments of the advance, incredible congestion occurred on the narrow road. Dismounted cavalry and infantry became entangled. The Rough Riders, led by Roosevelt, shoved and elbowed through ranks of sweating foot soldiers. Roosevelt's troopers pressed on followed by the balloon which sailed serenely overhead.

The Spaniards began shooting at the balloon with rifles and shrapnel. Shells raked the road and men went

Three U.S. generals commanding troops in Cuba. Brigadier-General Jacob Kent (top); Brigadier-General Henry W. Lawton (middle) and Brigadier-General Samuel S. Sumner (bottom). Sketch of General Sumner is by famed artist Frederic Remington.

79

Corpulent General William Shafter, accompanied by his
staff, pauses along El Caney trail to water horses on July 1.
Shafter rarely rode a horse because of his excessive
weight (above).

Spaniards fight from trenches and behind barbed wire
in effort to stem American attack on El Caney.
Vigorous Spanish resistance caused heavy casualties
among U.S. troops.

A unit of the 71st New York National Guard straggles across a shallow stream on the march to San Juan Hill. Conduct of regiment in battle brought criticism when some recruits refused to advance under enemy artillery fire.

Mists rise from jungle and forest over terrain which Americans traversed in crucial San Juan battle on July 1, 1898 (left). Note mountains in background.

Furious American charge has as its objective Spanish blockhouse (background) guarding approaches to El Caney (below).

Frederic Remington at San Juan

Mercaldo Archives

The noted American artist, Frederic Remington, was on spot during the Battle of San Juan. His sketches of action capture grimness of combat. Wounded men are carried to field hospital (top). Soldiers hit the dirt when enemy shells scream overhead. Litter bearers bring back wounded soldier. Slightly injured men, heading for dressing station, cheer ammunition train going towards front.

down. The shrieks of the wounded rattled the green troops and the Ist Battalion, 71st (New York) Infantry refused to advance. The New Yorkers, marching directly underneath the balloon, were caught by artillery in an open field near a ford across the San Juan River.

At last Spanish lead punctured the bag which sank gently to earth. Colonel Derby stepped out unharmed and the aerial phase of the war against Spain was over. Once the balloon had been knocked out, the enemy guns shifted to other targets and the 71st started to creep forward again.

First Lieutenant John J. Pershing, who commanded the U.S. Army in World War I, was an officer with the 10th (Negro) Cavalry. He described the march to San Juan Hill as a "hellish business."

Fighting Joe Wheeler, weakened by fever, dragged himself to the front and rode his horse into the middle of the shallow San Juan River. With bullets whizzing about, he waved the men on, shouting, "Keep moving! Keep moving! The damn Yankees can't stop us!"

Once again he had confused his wars.

The fighting at the base of Kettle Hill and San Juan Hill grew more intense. Colonel Charles Wikoff, commanding the 13th Infantry Regiment, was killed at the river. Men fell one after the other as the Spaniards fired from the safety of their blockhouses. Wounded men, trailing blood, staggered back to the dressing stations. The sight of those stumbling men further shook the raw troops who stared in mute horror.

Spanish prisoners taken at El Caney stand glumly in a field outside the village. Outnumbered, these Spaniards fought gamely until overwhelmed by superior American forces.

U.S. artillerymen dig in on hill near San Juan
prior to battle (left).

Crew of fieldpiece ducks blast of gun as it is
fired at Spanish positions on San Juan Hill.
U.S. artillery used in engagement were old-
fashioned and cumbersome. Black power smoke
soon obscured targets (above).

Map of San Juan and El Caney drawn by Caspar
Whitney shows course of action (left).

Lieutenant Colonel Teddy Roosevelt strikes a martial figure as he poses outside tent after Battle of San Juan. Roosevelt's vigorous leadership during the fighting earned him national renown and helped him win nomination on Republican ticket as Vice-President in 1900.

"Fighting Joe" Wheeler, second from left, holds council of war before San Juan battle. Although ailing from jungle fever, Wheeler got out of sick bed to take part in the fight (above).

Captain Bucky O'Neill, Troop H, Rough Riders, a famous western marshal from Arizona, believed an officer ought never take cover. "I'm here to lead my men, not to protect myself," he once had told Colonel Roosevelt. When the Rough Riders emerged from the jungle at the San Juan River, O'Neill stood erect and pointed at Kettle Hill. "Let's go get 'em boys! You'll find 'em up there!" he cried.

"Get down, captain!" a sergeant shouted. "You're in plain view . . ."

O'Neill grinned. "The Spanish bullet isn't made that will kill me." A moment later, he dropped, shot through the head.

Despite the gruelling fire being poured on them, the Americans grouped in attack formation. Infantry regulars under Lawton made for San Juan Hill while the discounted cavalry headed for Kettle Hill. The twin assault was launched at about 1:00 P.M.

Teddy Roosevelt galloped back and forth on his horse, Little Texas, rallying his Rough Riders. Beckoning them on, he spurred straight up Kettle Hill. Behind him came the Rough Riders and Negro troopers of the 10th Cavalry.

Shouting "Follow me!" Roosevelt began a ride that made him a national idol and led to the White House. His troopers ignored the Spanish guns and rushed upwards, gasping for breath, but never stopping.

Some 40 yards from the top of Kettle Hill (so named because of a huge iron sugar-refining kettle in the ruins of an old sugar mill on the hill's crest) the enemy had strung barbed wire. Roosevelt dismounted and Little Texas galloped off. At that instant, a bullet grazed the elbow of the future President, but Roosevelt crossed the wire, saber in one hand and a revolver in the other, while his panting troopers ran after him.

"They came on like a howling mob brandishing rifles . . . It was less a charge than a wild rush . . ." a newsman reported.

The enemy quit his trenches and fled to prepared positions. With an exultant yell, Rough Riders and Negro troopers swarmed atop Kettle Hill. At the same time, Lawton's infantry drove the Spanish from San Juan Hill. The Americans now held the key to Santiago—the ridges of the vital hills. They had won a precarious hold at high price. General Shafter winced when he learned that the victory had cost more than 1,000 dead

Mercaldo Archives

Teddy Roosevelt stands with some of his men on top of San Juan Hill. Rough Riders won glory by their fearless rush at height of battle.

and wounded.

There was much glory for Roosevelt and his Rough Riders, although professional soldiers sneered at his tactics. As the Rough Riders charged, a British Army observer, watching through binoculars made a wry face: "They've got courage to spare, but those are schoolboys playing a deadly game—not soldiers!"

For many of the Rough Riders atop Kettle Hill, more had been gained than the capture of an enemy position. The students, cowboys and city youths who made up the regiment had learned that the color of a man's skin made no difference.

One Rough Rider, Frank Knox, destined to be Secretary of the Navy in World War II, wrote his parents:

"I became separated from my unit but joined a troop of the 10th Cavalry, a Negro regiment, and for a time fought with them shoulder to shoulder, and in justice to the colored race I must say I never saw braver men anywhere . . ."

Frederic Remington's drawing captures final moments of wild Rough Rider charge up steep hill to storm Spanish position guarding crest (left).

BEHIND THE LINES

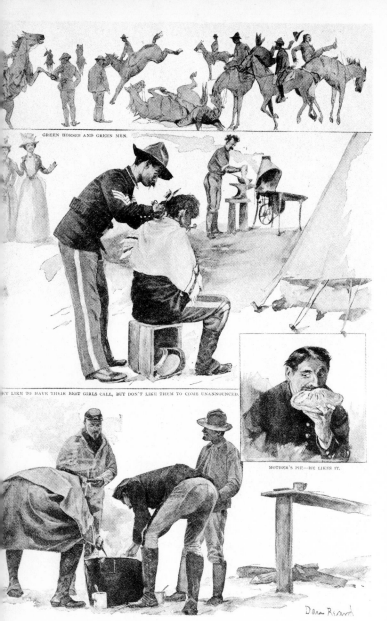

GREEN HORSES AND GREEN MEN.

RY LIKE TO HAVE THEIR BEST GIRLS CALL, BUT DON'T LIKE THEM TO COME UNANNOUNCED.

MOTHER'S PIE—HE LIKES IT.

Some of the joys and hardships of army life are shown in these sketches drawn at an unnamed training camp. Top picture depicts difficulties encountered by cavalry recruits trying to handle unbroken horses. Two young ladies (center) gaze in amusement at soldier getting his hair trimmed by a helpful amateur barber. Greedy rookie devours apple pie sent by his mother. Soldiers wash up mess kits after chow, a chore familiar to veterans of World War II. Soldiers (below) gather outside news correspondents tent to read latest bulletins posted on board.

A cold water tap provides washing up·
facilities for U.S. Army regulars at Camp
Black near Chickamauga, Ga. (top, left).
Enterprising news vendor (top, right)
supplies latest in reading matter for his
soldier-customers. The changing of
the guard (middle, left) is carried out in
the proper military manner. After-duty
hours barber shop is crude but well
equipped to trim whiskers in the fashion
of the day. Open field (bottom) serves
as campsite for 12th U.S. Infantry
Regiment. Soon after photograph was
taken, a tent city blossomed on this spot.

Cartoon depicts Uncle Sam testing sword blade (left) to symbolize nation's readiness for war. More explicit are these heavy coast defense mortars emplaced

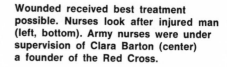

Wounded received best treatment possible. Nurses look after injured man (left, bottom). Army nurses were under supervision of Clara Barton (center) a founder of the Red Cross.

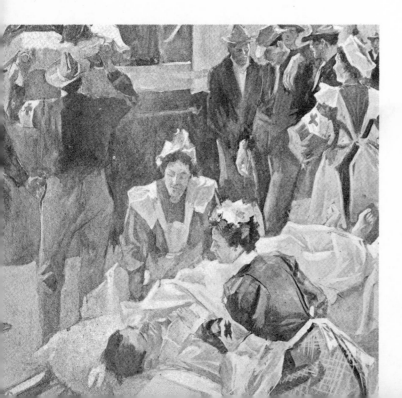

at Sandy Hook (center) and the steel foundry at Bethlehem, Pa. turning out armor plate for battleships.

Hospital corpsmen assist soldier from ambulance at casualty collecting station in Cuba. Naval surgeons operate in sick bay of warship. Note absence of gloves and masks on doctors and attendants. Unsanitary surgical procedures caused numerous deaths among servicemen.

Convalescent soldiers recovering
from tropical diseases sail back to
U.S. from Cuba aboard hospital
ship.

Red Cross worker serves coffee to haggard returnees
of U.S. V Corps. Men had contracted malaria, dysentery
and dengue fever in Cuban jungles. Rest camp was
established for them at Montauk Point, L.I., where
this transport has docked.

A soldier back from Cuba regales home town audience
with stirring tales of his adventures at the front.
It mattered little how accurate the stories might have
been. They merely had to be thrilling.

THE MEN, THE GUNS, THE TOOLS

Various uniforms of U.S. Army are shown here. In picture (left, top) the riflemen are U.S. regulars armed with Krag-Jorgensen rifles.
The bugler is a volunteer as indicated by stripes on trouser leg. Men (top, right) are New York National Guardsmen. They are equipped with knapsacks and

Springfield rifles. Note that Regulars use blanket roll and haversack. Horsemen (bottom, left) are typically rugged examples of volunteers who joined Rough Riders, adept with machete or revolver. Negro soldiers (bottom, right) are dismounted cavalry troopers. They are wearing (left to right) khaki tropical uniform, raincoat and blue winter uniform.

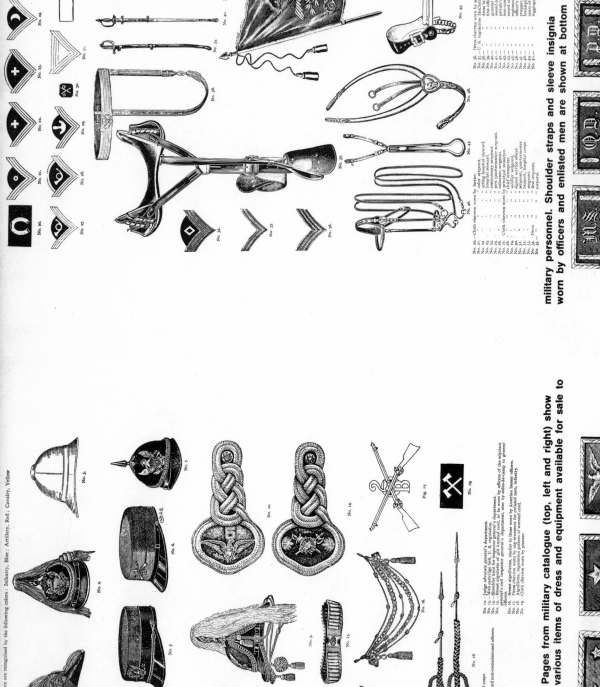

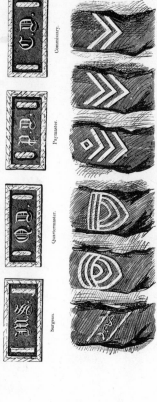

The different arms of the service are recognized by the following colors : Infantry, Blue ; Artillery, Red ; Cavalry, Yellow

No. 1.—Chapeau for officers of the general staff or staff corps.
No. 2.—Helmet, U. S. regulation for mounted troops.
No. 3.—Summer helmet, U. S. regulation, for infantry enlisted men.
No. 4.—Helmet for infantry enlisted men.
No. 5.—Regulation officer's cap.
No. 6.—New regulation cap for enlisted privates.
No. 7.—U. S. regulation for mounted troops.
No. 8.—U. S. regulation service hat.
No. 9.—Mounted officer's helmet.
No. 10.—Shoulder knot.
No. 11.—General's epaulette, U. S. regulation.
No. 12.—Judge advocate general's department.
No. 13.—Welt cartridge belt, U. S. regulation.
No. 14.—Shoulder knot for inspector general's department.
No. 15.—Breast aiguillette of gilt knotted cord, to be worn by officers of the adjutant general's and inspector general's department, also by aides-de-camp to general officers.
No. 16.—Breast aiguillette, similar to those worn by Austrian hussar officers.
No. 17.—Dress chevron worn by cap ornament for enlisted men, infantry.
No. 18.—Aiguillette, regulation pattern of worsted cord.
No. 19.—Cloth chevron worn by pioneer.

Pages from military catalogue (top, left and right) show various items of dress and equipment available for sale to military personnel. Shoulder straps and sleeve insignia worn by officers and enlisted men are shown at bottom

No. 20.—Cloth chevron worn by farrier.
No. 21.— " " " " color sergeant.
No. 22.— " " " " acting hospital steward.
No. 23.— " " " " hospital steward.
No. 24.— " " " " commissary sergeant.
No. 25.— " " " " post quartermaster sergeant.
No. 26.— " " " " sergeant-major.
No. 27.—Cloth chevron worn by principal musician.
No. 28.— " " " " chief trumpeter.
No. 29.— " " " " saddler sergeant.
No. 30.— " " " " signal service officer.
No. 31.— " " " " sergeant, quartermaster.
No. 32.— " " " " brassart, hospital corps.
No. 33.— " " " " first sergeant.
No. 34.—Dress " " " corporal.
No. 35.— " " " "

No. 36.—Dress chevron worn by sergeant.
No. 37.—U. S. regulation saddle.
No. 38.—Dress belt for line officers and general staff.
No. 39.—First officer of the navy, gilt mounts.
No. 40.—General officer's sword.
No. 41.—Cavalry officer's sword.
No. 42.—Private's saber for cavalry.
No. 43.—Saber for non-commissioned officers.
No. 44.—Sword of general staff.
No. 45.—Regimental colors for infantry, sword of medical or pay department.
No. 46.—Officer's bridle, eagle mounted rosettes.
No. 47.—Curb bit of polished steel.
No. 48.—Breastplate and martingales.
No. 49.—Spurs of polished gun metal.
No. 50.—Leggings of tan-colored duck.

Shoulder straps (left column, top to bottom): Commissary. Paymaster. Quartermaster. Surgeon.

Sleeve insignia (right column): Corporal. Second Sergeant. First or Orderly Sergeant. Quartermaster Sergeant. Hospital Steward.

Shoulder straps (officers): Colonel. Second Lieutenant. Brigadier-General. First Lieutenant. Major-General. Captain. Lieutenant General. Lieutenant-Colonel and Major.

Uniforms of Spanish Navy (top, left) include (l. to r.) marine, sailors, commander, executive officer, marine officer, seaman and gunner wearing fatigues. Army uniforms (middle, left) show infantryman, non-com, staff officer, General, lancer, infantry officer, cavalryman and field artilleryman.

Combat photograph shows Spanish infantrymen armed with Mauser rifles firing from trenches. Note barbed wire entanglements that have been set up in front of trench. Spaniards fought bravely, but leadership was bad and troops poorly trained.

Special troops (top to bottom) are Civil Guard, Volunteer and Mounted Scout.

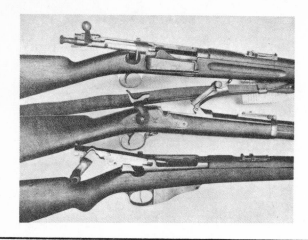

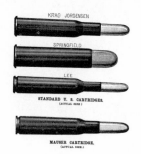

KRAG JORDENSEN

SPRINGFIELD

LEE

STANDARD U. S. CARTRIDGES.
(ACTUAL SIZE.)

MAUSER CARTRIDGE.
(ACTUAL SIZE.)

Ordnance used by American forces included (left) the Krag-Jorgensen rifle, the Springfield rifle and the Lee rifle which was used by the Navy. The machine gun (below) was the Colt Automatic Gun that could fire 400 shots per minute. Cross-sectional diagram (center, left) shows mechanism of Maxim machine gun which fired 750 rounds per minute. Cartridges (center, top) are for Krag-Jorgensen, Springfield and Lee. Fourth bullet is for Spanish Mauser rifle. Machine gun (below, left) capable of firing 300 one pound shells per minute, was for use on naval vessels. The 37 mm cannon (below, right) could be used on a naval mount or attached to carriage and limber (bottom) for employment ashore.

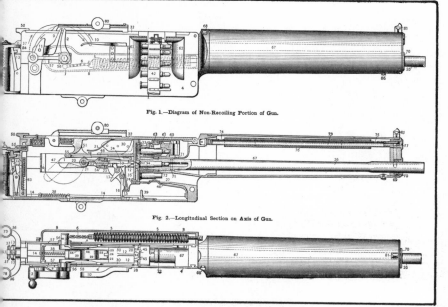

Fig. 1.—Diagram of Non-Recoiling Portion of Gun.

Fig. 2.—Longitudinal Section on Axis of Gun.

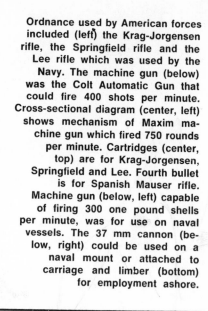

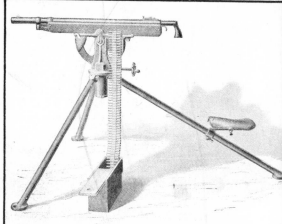

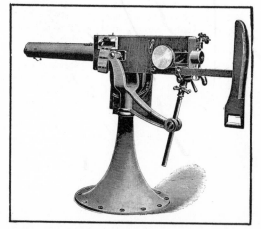

Gun carriage of Hotchkiss 2-pound mountain gun loaded on pack mule for transit to the front (top). Fletcher 3-inch rapid fire field guns are set up in artillery training camp. The Fletcher was noted for rapidity of fire and accuracy. Types of ammunition for Hotchkiss gun are (l. to r. left, below) armor-piercing shell, shrapnel, case shot, common shell and a complete cartridge with an armor-piercing shell. Ammunition for rapid fire guns (below, right) are (top to bottom) one pounder, 2½-pounder, 3-pounder 6-pounder, 9-pounder and 33-pounder, for a 4-inch naval gun. U.S. field artillery battery in action (bottom). Note gunner (left) ducking away from recoil blast.

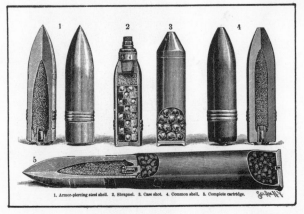

1. Armor-piercing steel shell. 2. Shrapnel. 3. Case shot. 4. Common shell. 5. Complete cartridge.

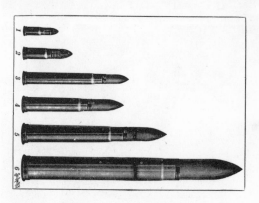

ADMIRAL

VICE-ADMIRAL

REAR ADMIRAL

COMMODORE

CAPTAIN

COMMANDER

LIEUTENANT-COMMANDER

LIEUTENANT

Uniforms and men of the U.S. Navy are seen in these pictures. Winter and summer type dress and working uniforms are worn by three sailors (top, left).
Men on right wear working clothes of naval gun crew.
Officers run sailors in fatigues through bayonet drill (above, left) while three U.S. Marines pose in tropical, winter and dress uniforms (above, right). Insignias of U.S. Navy Rank are illustrated at bottom, left.

Naval torpedoes were deadly, but highly erratic weapons in 1898. Sketch and cross-sectional drawing (right) shown working part of the Whitehead torpedo used by the U.S. Navy.

DIAGRAM SHOWING SEPARATE COMPARTMENTS OF THE WHITEHEAD AUTOMOBILE TORPEDO.

Machinists put finishing touches to torpedo in Spanish naval workshop, prior to installation aboard a warship.

Photograph (left) catches test launching of torpedo being shot out of tube such as those carried aboard torpedo-boat destroyers.

This realistic drawing shows the "Black Room" crew of a warship, where stokers toiled in fierce heat to feed the ship's fires and keep up a full head of steam.

Artist's version of battleship gun turret in action is highly romanticized view. Handling big gun on fighting ship was hard, noisy and dirty work. Seldom did an officer appear so nattily attired in full dress uniform, including parade sword.

Sailor on Spanish warship sighting a 4-inch rapid firing gun (left). Sketch appeared in American magazine shortly before outbreak of hostilities.

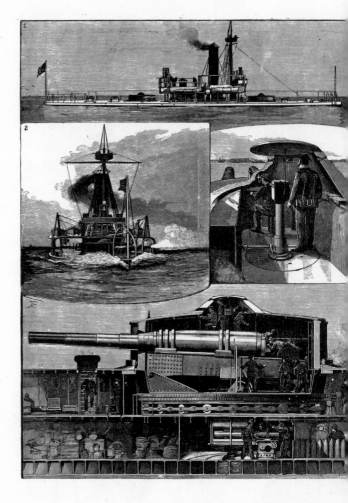

USS Miantonomoh, a Monitor class fighting ship is seen side view (top), moving at full speed (left, center). Interior of conning tower (center, right) shows deck officers guiding vessel. Cross-sectional view of turret and hull gives view of gun, loading devices and magazines.

Spanish sailors firing 6-pounder aboard gunboat. Drawing made in action off Cuba by Dutch artist.

Coast defense **Monitor** Amphitrite **carries 4-inch rapid-fire gun protected by a revolving shield.**

Crewmen polishing breech of powerful 13-inch gun aboard USS Iowa, **hard hitting battleship in the Atlantic Squadron.**

Loading devices for hauling shells from magazine to 13-inch gun turret on the USS Iowa. **Shells weigh several hundred pounds and must be handled by hoists.**

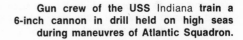

Gun crew of the USS Indiana **train a 6-inch cannon in drill held on high seas during maneuvres of Atlantic Squadron.**

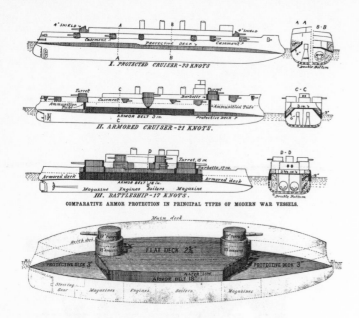

I. PROTECTED CRUISER—23 KNOTS.

II. ARMORED CRUISER—21 KNOTS.

III. BATTLESHIP—17 KNOTS.

COMPARATIVE ARMOR PROTECTION IN PRINCIPAL TYPES OF MODERN WAR VESSELS.

Cross-sectional diagram shows comparative armored protection in war vessels of 1898 vintage. From top to bottom, a protected cruiser—with speed of 23 knots; an armored cruiser, top speed 21 knots, battleship, maximum speed, 17 knots. Bottom sketch shows battleship as an "invulnerable floating fort."

Men of coast defense Monitor Amphitrite stand beneath forward pair of 10-inch guns which constitute the vessel's principal armament.

Drawing shows various underwater and submarine devices used in naval warfare of 1898. Note midget submarine firing miniature torpedo, and assorted types of mines.

THE NAVIES CLASH–July 3, 1898

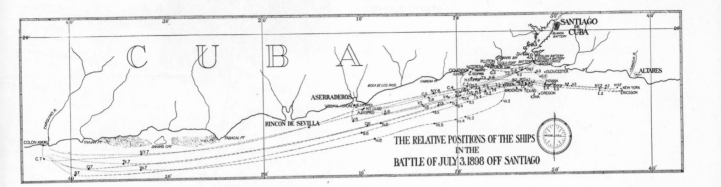

THE RELATIVE POSITIONS OF THE SHIPS
IN THE
BATTLE OF JULY 3,1898 OFF SANTIAGO

When darkness came that momentous July 1, Fighting Joe Wheeler, who had resumed his place as senior commander at the front, sent an alarming message to El Pozo, where Shafter's command post was located. The ex-Confederate said in part:

> ". . . our lines are stretched thin . . . I hope more men can be brought up . . . I believe we can hold tomorrow against a counterattack . . . but I fear it will be a very severe day . . ."

When this was shown to fever-wracked Shafter, the General groaned, "I don't know whether we've gained a victory or brought on a disaster . . ."

He need not have been so pessimistic. Although the lines on the hilltops were lightly held, the troops clung to their positions despite heavy Spanish shelling the next day.

Shafter pondered his next move. The enemy was before him in far stronger positions than those that had been so bloodily captured. A frontal assault would have cost many lives and Shafter was reluctant to risk his men. A siege was preferable, but time was running out. Disease was rampant in the Vth Corps and any hour a hurricane might strike, cutting the American lines of communication. Shafter appealed to Admiral Sampson for the fleet to enter Santiago Harbor and bombard the city with the ships' big guns.

The Admiral refused to follow this course. He made vague excuses about mines endangering his ships. Instead Sampson told Shafter that he would come to Siboney on Sunday, July 3, aboard the *New York* for a conference to work out a strategy which would ". . . expedite the capture of Santiago with the least effusion of American blood . . ."

Captain Robley "Fighting Bob" Evans, commanding the battleship USS Iowa gave alarm when Spanish fleet tried to escape from Santiago harbor on July 3, 1898. Iowa was first U.S. ship in action.

Commodore Winfield Scott Schley was temporarily in command of the U.S. Atlantic Squadron on Sunday, July 3, when the Spanish fleet made its futile dash for freedom. Drawing shows Schley on bridge of his flagship USS Brooklyn, as American ships speed in pursuit of fleeing enemy vessels.

President William Mc Kinley, surrounded by cabinet members and aides, scans latest despatches from Cuba on that fateful Sunday when naval battle of Santiago was joined and outcome of war hung in balance.

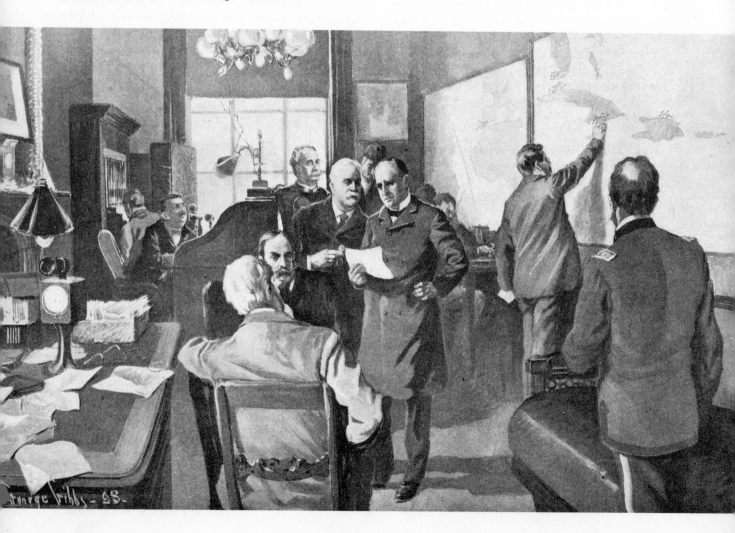

Cuban insurrectos take grisly revenge on their Spanish oppressors. Rifle toting rebels crouch on beach near Santiago to shoot survivors attempting escape from sinking Spanish warships. Bodies of two Spanish sailors lie sprawled on rocky shore (left).

Sunday, July 3, found the Americans still entrenched on the hills. Shafter waited at Siboney for Sampson's arrival. At 9:35 A.M., the battleship *New York* was observed cruising slowly towards shore. Cubans and Americans crowded the sands to watch the big ship's approach. All at once, everyone heard the booming of big naval guns beyond the hills at the entrance to Santiago Harbor. Sampson, on the bridge of his flagship, realized those guns could only mean that the Spanish fleet was trying to break out.

The Admiral ordered the *New York* to put about at full speed. As she swung in a wide circle, he could dimly make out the Spanish flagship, *Maria Teresa,* racing from the harbor mouth toward the blockading ships and the open sea.

Admiral Pacual Cervera y Topete, in full dress uniform of rank. He had predicted doom of his fleet.

Panoramic sketch shows ships of Spanish and U.S. fleets
off Santiago, Cuba on Sunday morning, July 3, 1898.
At left, the cruiser Brooklyn and the battleships Texas and
Oregon pursue the Cristobal Colon and the Vizacaya.

At right, the Almirante Oqueno and the Infanta Maria Teresa are aflame after pounding by big guns of USS Iowa (center). The American cruiser Gloucester is seen (foreground) closing in for the kill.

Terrible effect of USS Iowa's 13-inch guns can be seen on the scarred and battered hulk of the Spanish cruiser Vizcaya which suffered fatal damage. Men on deck are American salvage experts.

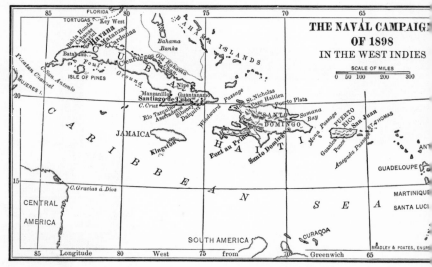

THE NAVAL CAMPAIGN OF 1898 IN THE WEST INDIES

Spanish seamen taken prisoners of war at the battle of Santiago were transported to Seavey's Island, Portsmouth, New Hampshire. The lucky survivors of Vizcaya and Cristobal Colon are having their names checked by Captain Emilio Diaz Mareau, skipper of the Cristobal Colon.

When Sampson left for Siboney, Commodore Winfield Scott Schley, aboard the *Brooklyn,* succeeded to temporary command of the blockading squadron. As the *Maria Teresa,* flying the flag of Admiral Cervera, came into the open, a lookout on the battleship U.S.S. *Iowa* sounded the alarm. Captain Robley D. Evans, the *Iowa's* skipper made for the bridge at a dead run. He gaped in wonderment as he saw the *Maria Teresa* heading his way, followed by the rest of Cervera's fleet —the cruisers *Vicazaya, Cristobal Colon, Almirante Oquenda* and the torpedo boat destroyers *Furor* and *Pluton.*

The oncoming ships were immediately spotted by the blockading vessels. Signals flashed; men dashed to battle stations; gunners peered through range finders and below decks, fireroom crews worked feverishly to get up steam. Commodore Schley raised the signals "Clear for action!" and "Engage the enemy!"

At 9:35 A.M., the *Maria Teresa* opened fire and her captain, Victor M. Concas, turned to Admiral Cervera. "Poor Spain! My poor Spain!" he said with tears in his eyes. "This is her last bid for glory . . ."

The American guns returned the shots. In an unbelievably short time almost every Spanish ship was either aflame, sinking or beached. When a broadside from the *Texas* set off explosions on the *Vicazaya,* the American gunners raised a triumphant shout and an officer admonished, "Don't cheer, boys! The poor devils are dying!"

The only Spanish ship to escape swift destruction was the fast cruiser *Cristobal Colon* which reached open water as the fleet was pounded to pieces. She sped for Havana with Americans in pursuit. At 1:00 P.M., the *Oregon* came close enough to use her 13-inch

Officer aboard USS *Texas* cries, "Don't cheer boys, the poor devils are dying!" as American broadside sets *Vizacaya* ablaze.

guns. Rather than have his ship blown to bits, the master of the *Cristobal Colon* ran her aground some 50 miles from Santiago.

The naval battle of Santiago was over. The Spanish fleet was destroyed.

Sampson was irked that Schley, whom he disliked had been in charge during the fight. When Schley signaled the *New York,* "We have gained a great victory," Sampson ungraciously demanded, "Report your casualties."

On that subject Schley reported one man killed and one man wounded. The enemy suffered 323 killed and 1,813 captured.

It had been a great day for the Americans, a fine Fourth of July present to the nation.

Men of USS *Oregon* raise triumphant shout as speedy Spanish warship *Cristobal Colon* is beached after long chase during which enemy vessel seemed to be outdistancing the mighty *Oregon.*

THE FALL OF SANTIAGO—July 16, 1898

The death of the Spanish fleet doomed Santiago. To celebrate Independence Day, speakers stressed the grand prospects facing the U.S. Cuba was all but conquered and, in time, by a solemn pledge, would be turned over to the Cubans. But no one mentioned anything about letting go of the Philippines and there was Puerto Rico for the taking, along with the Spanish-owned Canary Islands or the Balearics.

An imperialist spokesman declared: "The sweep of war is like a whirlwind . . . no man can tell where it will reach . . ."

This was the tone and temper of the time. The Yellow Press backed it to the limit. The U.S. was firmly on the path of imperialism and took a giant step toward becoming a colonial power by annexing Hawaii on July 7 against the token opposition of 15 Democrats and one Republican in the Senate.

Aerial sketch shows Santiago and the surrounding countryside just before naval battle. Note American positions at Siboney and Daiquiri (left). U.S. ships are seen blockading Santiago Harbor, (background), while bottled up Spanish vessels lie at anchor in the channel.

Corned "willy" and hard tack, standard emergency rations in the U.S. Army of 1898, are brought up to frontline troops holding positions in the hills near Santiago. Despite poor food, men's spirits are high as they prepare to eat.

Cuban partisans join in push across railroad tracks
near Santiago, supporting advance of Second
U.S. Infantry Regiment.

Hard fighting American riflemen storm hilltop
Spanish entrenchments with fixed bayonets during
assault on enemy strongholds defending Santiago.

Surprise Spanish night attack almost overwhelmed
American outpost in the vicinity of Santiago. Artist Howard
Chandler Christy's drawing depicts fierce defense by
U.S. Army regulars. Bursting grenade causes casualty. Note
ammunition carrier bringing up case of ammunition
for Krag-Jorgensen rifles being used by Americans on
firing line.

Steam launch (center) and long boats from U.S. transports
carrying troops under General Nelson A. Miles towards
mountanious shore of Porto Rico as invasion of that Spanish-
held island gets underway on July 25, 1898.

Dark lines on map of Porto Rico (left) indicate
route of American invaders during their
march across the island. Original landings
were made near Ponce. Other troops
fanned out to the west and took Mayaguez
while the main force cut across to San Juan
in the northern section of Porto Rico.

Cuban and American officers hold conference
at U.S. command post outside Santiago.
General William Shafter, American
commanding officer, is seen at left consulting
with high ranking Cuban. White-bearded
man in center is General Joseph Wheeler

114

Insurgents waylay a Spanish troop train somewhere in Porto Rico to prevent reinforcements from reaching the front. Americans were aided by such partisan activity during the course of the brief campaign.

Negro troops guard batch of enemy prisoners taken in battle during U.S. advance across the island.

That same day, General Nelson A. Miles boarded a train for Tampa where he would take command of several volunteer regiments earmarked for the invasion of Puerto Rico. At about the very time—7:00 P.M.—McKinley was signing the Hawaiian Treaty, a remarkable scene took place in the hills outside Santiago. General Shafter had completed arrangements with General Jose Toral, who now commanded the Santiago garrison (Linares had been wounded) to exchange Lieutenant Hobson and the *Merrimac* volunteers for 20 captured Spanish officers.

Hobson and his men, riding in an open wagon, passed through the American outposts down the long, crowded road to the beach. All the way, cheering soldiers greeted the heroes. A regimental band serenaded the *Merrimac* men on the beach and warships fired blank salutes. Hobson was taken aboard the *New York* where he cheerfully recounted his story to newsmen.

General Nelson A. Miles pauses to chat with aide as his troops push on towards San Juan.

Two U.S. soldiers guard prisoners (left) rounded up after a skirmish during the Porto Rican fighting. Spanish put up only desultory resistance.

American troops march into Mayaguez, Porto Rico. Disarmed Spaniards had attempted to flee, but were captured after a hard chase by victorious Yanks.

Mercaldo Archives

Message announcing end of Porto Rican hostilities is delivered to U.S. artillery general near Guayama, just as orders were about to be given for commencement of bombardment.

Sharpest fighting in Porto Rico was at Ceame, north-east of Ponce. Spaniards stubbornly resisted in jungle-covered mountains. Note native straw-thached houses on left.

Mercaldo Archives

On July 17, 1898, General Jose Toral, commanding the Spanish forces in Santiago, Cuba, surrendered his army to General William Shafter (center, right) as officers and men of both sides look on. The capitulation of Santiago virtually ended the Cuban phase of the Spanish-American War.

That hot July, the country was happy and well pleased. Rumors arose that Spain was seeking an armistice. According to Teddy Roosevelt, "It was a grand time to be alive! A bully time!"

After long negotiations, General Toral surrendered Santiago on July 16. The Spanish capitulations came at the right moment for heavy rains were ruining American communication lines; with the wet season, the malaria rate rose alarmingly. Shafter grunted with relief as he concluded the surrender.

But with the fall of Santiago, new problems confronted the Army. Yellow fever threatened at Siboney while malaria laid low more than 5,000 men of the Vth Corps. Fortunately, the war in Cuba was virtually over. On July 18, the Spanish Ambassador to France asked the French government to help negotiate a truce. On that day, Miles chafing at the inactivity, in Cuba, received permission from the War Department to invade Puerto Rico and "raise the American flag."

On another part of the Santiago front, Spanish officer with bearer carrying flag of truce, salutes smartly as he delivers surrender to U.S. officer.

General Jose Toral, Spanish commander
at Santiago, poses for portrait in full
dress uniform. A courageous officer, Toral
realized further resistance was futile
after destruction of Cervera's fleet fleet
on July 3, 1898.

Proclamation in Spanish announces U.S.
occupation of Santiago listing regulations
pertaining to the government of the
conquered territory as drawn up by President
William Mc Kinley.

A week later, Miles put a force of 3,300 volunteers
ashore at Guanica; three days later, more U.S. troops
swarmed off transports near Ponce. Both landings
were unopposed and Puerto Ricans greeted the *Yanquis* with joy. Less than a month after his arrival, Miles
had conquered Puerto Rico, his troops went home and
the island was securely in American hands.

Friday, August 12, 1898, at 4:30 P.M., less than

four months after war had been declared, Secretary of
State William R. Day and the French Ambassador,
Jules Cambron, acting on behalf of Spain signed a
peace protocol ending all hostilities. President Mc
Kinley immediately proclaimed an armistice and the
nation went on a binge of wild celebration. Schools
were closed, church bells rang and crowds danced in
the streets.

The war was over!

American troops entrenched outside Santiago demonstrate
their joy when news of the city's surrender reached the front.
Many of the cheering soldiers were suffering from
malaria and other tropical diseases. Sickness caused more
casualties than did Spanish bullets.

Monsieur Jules Cambon, French Ambassador to Spain, acting on that country's request, signed an armistice ending the Spanish-American War. Ceremony took place in Washington on Friday, August 12, 1898. President William Mc Kinley, second from left, looked on. William D. Day (center) was American signatory.

U.S. officers and enlisted men watch Stars and Stripes being raised above the Municipal Building in Santiago, Cuba. Cutout letters hailing King Alfonso XIII of Spain still stand on structure.

THE PHILLIPPINE INSURRECTION 1898-1902

There was an ugly aftermath to the Spanish-American War which Secretary of State John Hay (who succeeded Day) called "the splendid little war."

The brave and long suffering Filipinos who had fought so hard for independence against Spain, were turned over to the U.S. by the terms of the peace treaty between Spain and America. American sovereignty in the islands was bought at the price of $20,000,000 which was paid to Spain for the Philippines. Now, the 10,000,000 Filipinos belonged to Uncle Sam.

Spaniards, residing in Manila, formed troops of volunteers. This company, typical of the rest, was manned by members of exclusive Casino Club.

View of village in Philippines was familiar to American soldiers. Thousands of such small settlements dotted the islands.

On night of February 4, 1898, insurrectos under Emilio Aguinaldo attacked American troops near Manila. This was signal for general uprising against Americans. Disappointment at delay in granting Philippine independence sparked the insurrection.

Filipino insurgents, lined up in military manner, pose for photograph on street in outskirts of Manila. Men such as these, although untrained, fought bravely against U.S. forces seeking to suppress their bid for independence.

121

In 1875, the U.S. received trading rights in Hawaii, and twelve years later was granted permission by the native Queen Lilikuolani, to build a naval base at Pearl Harbor, Honolulu. However, strong sentiment existed within the U.S. to take over the "Pineapple Paradise". A U.S.-inspired revolt overthrew the Queen in 1893 and by 1898, Hawaii was annexed as a territory by the U.S. Photograph shows ceremony on August 2, 1898, held in Honolulu, to ratify annexation. Tall man with white beard is Sanford Dole, president of Hawaii, who set up independent republic after Queen Lili-kuolani had been deposed. Methods Americans used in gaining territory had met with success earlier in 19th Century in California and Texas.

Although never granted independence, Aguinaldo's followers had set up all the machinery of government including newspapers (top, left and right); postage stamps (center, left); banknotes (lower, right) and even held a victory banquet to celebrate independence. Banquet menu cover (above, left) bears imprint of flag of Philippine Republic.

However, Aguinaldo and his *amigos* fought as desperately against the *Yanquis* as they had the Spanish. The anti-American struggle took the lives of 250,000 Filipino civilians who died from hunger and disease while another 20,000 fell in combat. The war that nobody wanted or foresaw cost the U.S. 5,000 battle fatalities and 3,000 wounded. Several thousand more Americans contracted tropical diseases which later brought untimely death to many. In this ignored and forgotten conflict the U.S. employed 60,000 troops and spent over $600,000,000 to subdue the rebellious Filipinos in fighting that lasted from 1899 until 1902.

The revolt in the Philippines was finally suppressed when a daredevil colonel from Kansas named Fredrick Funston captured Aguinaldo. At last the Stars and Stripes could fly over the Philippines. The American people should have been well pleased with their new Empire, but 250,000 Filipino corpses somehow tarnished their satisfaction.

Cartoons (top, right and center) comment on aspects of the situation in the Philippines. Upper cartoon shows indignant Uncle Sam preparing to chop barbed plant labelled "Cruelty in the army." Unbiased investigators proved that U.S. forces were guilty of wanton cruelty against Filipinos. Middle cartoon shows frustrated German Kaiser, Wilhelm II, who also sought to take Philippines.

WILLIAM, YOU'RE TOO LATE.

Old-fashioned cannon is mounted by insurgents to dominate single track railroad used by American troops. Despite obsolete weapons, Filipinos waged costly guerilla war against Americans for three years.

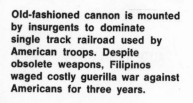

Furious fighting raged during Philippine
insurrection. In this battlefield drawing by
Frederic Remington, U.S. infantrymen
swarm over insurgent positions in bayonet
attack such as those against Spaniards during
Cuban campaign.

American patrol sloshes through jungle
swamp in search for elusive insurrectos who
conducted masterly guerilla type warfare.

Crude bamboo bridge built by U.S. Army
engineers spans river to replace structure
blown up by retreating insurgents.

American troops pour volley fire into jungle where it is believed insurgents are hidden (top left). Although Aguinaldo's men were brilliant at hit-and-run warfare, their luck sometimes ran out. Pictures (right and center) show dead rebels shot down by Americans.

American engineers toil in tropical heat to repair demolished railroad bridge blown up by insurrectos to delay U.S. pursuers.

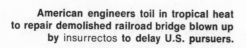

Brigadier General Arthur MacArthur (upper right) commanded U.S. forces in the Philippines. He was father of famed General Douglas MacArthur.

Doughty Brigadier General Frederick Funston, wearing the sunflower of his native Kansas, is photographed aboard transport Tartar after reutrn from Philippines. Funston won hight acclaim for his daring feat in capturing Aguinaldo (shown right with group of officers). Funston's dashing deed brought insurrection to an end.

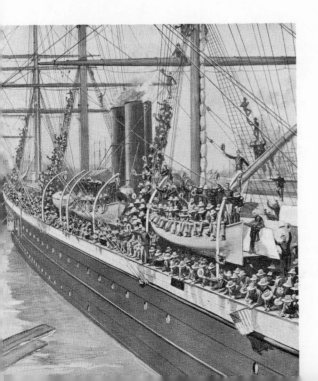

Homebound Yanks line ship rails as their vessel pulls into San Francisco after arduous duty in suppressing the Filipinos and securing that territory for the United States (right).

127

As the nation entered the 20th Century, Admiral Mahan made an astute observation: "The jocund youth of our people now passes away never to return . . . The cares and anxieties of manhood's years henceforth are ours . . ."

The "splendid little war" of 1898, its heroes and villains have been obscured in the hectic events of the passing years. But what happened in 1898 brought the end of an era to America. It was then that she reached the turning point and came of age. Grown to reluctant maturity, she became a nation responsible not only to herself but to the entire world.

Amidst fireworks and thunderous applause, New York City hails end of Spanish-American war and celebrates visit of Admiral Dewey to city. Note illuminated sign on Brooklyn Bridge. None of the city's thousands could then know that the U.S. had embarked on a path that would lead into two World Wars and bloody commitments in such distant places as Korea and Vietnam. America had come of age.